TOTAL QUALITY MANAGEMENT

Reports From The Front Lines

James L. Truesdell

Smith Collins

Publisher's Cataloging-in-Publication Data

Truesdell, James L., 1949
          Total quality management : reports from the front lines /
James L. Truesdell — 1st ed.
St. Louis, MO : Smith Collins Co., © 1994
          p.   cm.
          Includes index.
          ISBN: 0-9623414-9-5

          1. Total quality management   I. Title.

HD62.15.T78 1994   658.5 dc20

Printed in the United States of America

For Gayle . . .

And our children,
Jason, Daniel, Christy, Mindy,
Adam, Emily, and Sarah

Contents

Aspects Of Quality

Acknowledgements

The author expresses his thanks to the many individuals who consented to be interviewed for this work and without whose valuable contributions the book could not have been completed. Special thanks to Linda Watson for her assistance in typing significant portions of the manuscript and to Gayle Truesdell and Jean Ann Afflerbach for help in proofreading.

Additionally, thanks to the publishers and staff of *The Quality Observer*, *Distributor Magazine*, *The Distributor's Link*, *The Surplus Record*, *Service Reporter*, and the employees of Brauer Supply Company.

Publisher Gary Gardiner of Smith Collins provided advice, encouragement, and thoughtful critiques. Curt Neitzke lent his creative talents to the book's cover and design. Thanks also to Kate Bandos of KSB Promotions.

The book represents the cumulative efforts of these many people who made its preparation not only easier, but an enjoyable experience as relationships were formed or strengthened in the process.

James L. Truesdell
April 1994

Preface

This book speaks to the manager just embarking on the road to a Total Quality program and to those in the midst of the process who are seeking a road map to success. It shares my own experiences in getting a quality process off the ground at a midwestern distribution business and taps into a network of CEO's, quality managers, and consultants to examine the many facets of Total Quality Management in practical application.

Through the chapters which follow, the reader will find encouragement from those in large and small businesses who are committed to raising the quality level of their products and services and will learn of various techniques and concepts which have been used effectively.

This is not a technical book and here will not be found statistical formulas or mathematical equations to increase production or maximize profit. Here you will listen to thoughts and sense the excitement of men and women who are filled with an evangelical zeal for a cause which they are convinced will be not only a catalyst for their own company's success, but an impetus for their country's rise to the top of the new international marketplace.

Stepping out on the road to Total Quality can be a lonely experience.

In the Spring of 1991, fresh from a two-day seminar hosted by the Northamerican Heating, Refrigeration and Air Conditioning Wholesalers Association and Honeywell, Inc. I returned to Brauer Supply Company in St. Louis "on fire" with the idea of implementing a quality program at our seven locations in Missouri and Illinois.

Despite the intensive training at the seminar I was fully aware that "quality" had an intrinsically intangible nature and that every company's management would have to determine just what it constituted for themselves and for their customers.

While several "gurus" have been widely accepted and followed as guiding theorists of the quality revolution, it is clear that each company in each market situation must map out its own course and select those features and structures which fit best within its own culture.

The topics addressed in this book focus on specific issues growing out of the quality process and we take a look at their impact on the various constituencies involved—owners, managers, employees, vendors, and most importantly the customers of an organization.

We will look at the implementation of a process from the decision by management to pursue the quality objective through the development of a policy, designation of a steering committee, and the surveying of internal and external customers. The obstacles and roadblocks faced will be examined and suggestions made for overcoming these problems.

Most importantly, the reader will join in a dialogue with dozens of managers on the front line of quality as they outline the steps they have taken at their companies, in partnership with senior management, to enlist everyone within and without their organization in the drive for Total Quality. The need for full commitment and a revision of our old perspective on acceptable work processes will become apparent.

We will see how companies are restructuring their employee training to emphasize response to customer needs and how projects are tackled by self-directed teams of workers. The role played by suppliers, consultants and outside professionals in helping a company focus on quality will be examined as well as goal-setting and reward systems. Current economic trends such as the increasing use of temporary employees and the impact of emerging social and environmental concerns will be juxtaposed against the growing backdrop of the quality movement. The means of bringing the varied interests into harmony will be discussed.

After sharing stories of success and failure—what has worked and what has not—we will walk together through a series of steps to form a "Quality Action Plan" which can be applied to any business, regardless of size or structure.

Large businesses in the United States currently find themselves swept up in a blizzard of paperwork and procedures as they respond to pressures from their competitors and customers to get on board the quality bandwagon. In many instances this is channeled into efforts to win the Malcolm Baldrige Award or to gain certification to the ISO 9000 standard. These no doubt are effective motivators for quality and provide goals toward which the efforts of an organization can be directed.

The basic principles of Total Quality are, however, well within the reach of any organization regardless of resources or numbers of people. In fact, it is in the small organization where the commitment and personality strength of the CEO are most critical.

Yes. Starting out on the road to quality can be a lonely experience. I have stood before a room full of skeptical employees and tried to describe just what it was we were about to undertake and have struggled to win converts from line workers and union leaders whose expressions and body language radiated skepticism. I have felt pangs of embarrassment when a customer, quite rightfully, has angrily flung back our loudly trumpeted "commitment to quality" after we had dropped the ball on an important delivery. I have questioned the depth of my own commitment and follow through when economic recession and intense competition led me to "lay low" on the process at the very time efforts should have been stepped up.

At such times it was the knowledge that I was part of something bigger than just myself, or Brauer Supply Company, that prompted me to get back on track. It was clear that, throughout America, the quality movement was growing and people were standing up and moving their companies forward in this area at an increasing pace. In fact, as more and more of our customers began placing formal quality demands upon us it became easier to "sell" our own employees on the concept. Clearly, some of our larger corporate customers were telling us "Get in line with TQM if you wish to continue to be our business partner!"

Hopefully you, the reader, will gain some of that same sense of the quality imperative from the ideas and thoughts developed in this collection of essays, many of which were originally published in *The Quality Observer, The International News Magazine of Quality.*

They have been modified and molded together with much new material to provide a forum for a dialogue with those around the country who are struggling to make TQM a reality.

To those considering beginning a quality process, I heartily urge you to join the movement! To those who have already jumped in with both feet, it is my hope that you will find reassurance, strength, and support from my experiences and those of others who will speak to you through these pages.

Cast of Contributors

Edward C. Andler—Author of *Winning The Hiring Game* and President of Certified Reference Checking, St. Louis, Missouri

Karin M. Barker—Director of Employee Training and Development for Maritz, Inc., St. Louis, Missouri

Robert A. Barnett—Vice President of London Metal Services, Inc., London, Ontario

Robert A. Beck—Quality Assurance Manager of Amana Refrigeration, Inc., Fayetteville, Tennessee

William Beck—Vice President of Precisionaire, Inc., St. Petersburg, Florida

Michael Berry—Area Quality Manager of Southwestern Bell Telephone, St. Louis, Missouri

Kenneth Best—Vice President for Quality Systems of McDonnell Douglas Corporation, St. Louis, Missouri

James Boldt—former Director of Elementary and Secondary Education of the Lutheran Church-Missouri Synod, St. Louis, Missouri

Cay Bradley—Quality Coach for Wholesale Distribution Industry group of IBM, Atlanta, Georgia

Duane Brinkman—Director of Management Services for The Principal Financial Group, Des Moines, Iowa

Russell G. Broeckelmann—President of Coastline Distribution, Inc., Sanford, Florida, and founder of consultant Precision Distribution Systems

Sharon B. Canter—Director of Strategic Information for Manpower Temporary Services, Milwaukee, Wisconsin

Scott D. Dickerhoff—Senior Product Development Engineer and Quality Improvement Team Facilitator for anesthesiology division of Mallinkrodt Medical, Inc., St. Louis, Missouri

Keith R. Dierberg—Instructor in Management of Concordia University of Mequon, Wisconsin

David M. Draga—Vice President of Indiana Supply Corporation, Indianapolis, Indiana

Barbara Drago—Vice President of Boatmen's National Bank, St. Louis, Missouri

Patrick Geary—President of Geary Pacific Corporation, Anaheim, California

David B. Gleason—President of Systematic Selling, Inc., Islip, New York

Thomas E. Good—3M Quality Management Services, St. Paul, Minnesota

Jay L. Hepler—Sales Manager of A-1 Compressor, Inc., Indianapolis, Indiana

John R. Hohenstein—Supervisor of Credit and Collections-National Accounts of United Van Lines, St. Louis, Missouri

Jeffrey W. Holmes—Quality Assurance Manager of Airguard Industries, Inc., Louisville, Kentucky

Stan C. Hurt—President of Indiana Supply Corporation, Indianapolis, Indiana

John J. Irace—President of Packaging Concepts, Inc., St. Louis, Missouri

Robert Irwin—Vice President of Quality for Sverdrup Corporation, St. Louis, Missouri

Stanley G. Jones—District Customer Service Manager for United Parcel Service, Earth City, Missouri

Donald Kardux—President of consulting firm Business Navigators, Toledo, Ohio

Terrence J. Korpal—retired U.S. Secret Service Agent and President of Korpal & Associates, St. Louis, Missouri

Jo Ellen Lemmon—Quality Assurance Supervisor for Parker-Kalon Division of Black & Decker, Campbellsville, Kentucky

J. Richard Mansell—Director of Sales & Marketing of Cleveland Stamping, Cleveland, Ohio

Donald L. Miller—President of Superior Supply Company, Kansas City, Missouri

Richard C. Mues—Regional Vice President and Manager of Engineering for Kuether and Associates, St. Louis, Missouri and Tampa, Florida

Patrick Openlander—Psychologist in private practice and former faculty member of Washington University and St. Louis University, St. Louis, Missouri

Michael Orso—Vice President of General Data Systems, St. Louis, Missouri

Jerry Peterson—President of Mortemp, Inc., Seattle, Washington

Charles Reaves—former Sales Manager of A T & T and founder of consultants Twenty-One Associates, Atlanta, Georgia

Kevin Richeson—Assistant Director of Human Resources, Ritz-Carlton Hotel of St. Louis, Missouri

Kimberly Starr Rist—Director of Human Resources, Ritz-Carlton Hotel of St. Louis, Missouri

Jerry Shafer—Vice President of Sales for Consolidated Industries Corporation, Lafayette, Indiana

Peter W. Schutz—former CEO of Porsche AG Worldwide, now consultant and lecturer on management topics, Naples, Florida

Kenneth Sisson—President of Mid-Way Supply, Zion, Illinois

Joseph Stager—Distribution Sales and Product Manager of Atlas Bolt and Screw Co., Ashland, Ohio

Joseph Steiner—President of the Office Interiors Division of Color Art, Inc., St. Louis, Missouri

Scott Stratman—Director of Special Markets, R & D Systems, Colorado Springs, Colorado

Thomas Tener—Vice President of Maritz Motivation Company, St. Louis, Missouri

Arlie J. Thayer—Vice President for Corporate Quality Assurance at Panduit Corporation, Tinley Park, Illinois

Kenneth Urbanski—Vice President of Haber Operations, Detroit, Michigan

Janet Varner—Senior Project Manager for Research, Boatmen's Bancshares, St. Louis, Missouri

James M. Wall—President of Quality Business Forms, Inc., St. Louis, Missouri

Leo B. Walsh—President of Columbus Temperature Control, Columbus, Ohio

Dave Whiting—President of General Data Systems, Inc., St. Louis, Missouri

James R. Widtfeldt—Manager of Quality Education for Honeywell Home and Building Controls, Golden Valley, Minnesota

Steven A. Wikstrom—Vice President of Manufacturing of Reell Precision Manufacturing, St. Paul, Minnesota

Powell Woods—former Vice President of Human Resources and Community Relations for Nestle USA, Cleveland, Ohio

Marguerite M. Yonda—independent computer consultant of Computer Solutions, Rochester, New York

1

Why Quality?

Little by little, it creeps almost unseen into an organization.

People stop doing the little things that helped the successful company establish its place in the market. The supervisor on the production line lets an item pass on to shipping despite the fact that its shape is slightly out of alignment. The customer service person decides to wait until tomorrow to call the customer back. The purchasing department waits to order that special item for a customer until the next regular stock order is run. The sales manager tolerates a decrease in the number of customer contacts by good old Charlie because he dislikes the idea of a confrontation.

These and dozens of other little events add up to a sense of complacency that undermines a company's morale and inevitably erodes the customer base. All through the organization people and systems are failing the test at the moment of truth when the customer's needs must be met.

Somewhere else there is a competitor whose people are energized and who has systems in place to ensure that quality service and products are delivered consistently and on time. Its people will go the extra mile to figure out what it is the customer wants and then move heaven and earth to give that customer exactly what that is and then some.

This outfit will eat the first company's lunch!

While the first company has slipped into complacency, the second has developed a culture where quality service is the expected norm and anything less will not be tolerated by management or co-workers.

To a certain extent the United States and other traditional industrialized nations have found themselves in the position of the first company described. The world economy was our oyster following World War II. There was seemingly very little we could do to lose our market. Customers were literally lined up to buy and it became easy to develop bad habits and disregard the basics of what a quality company should be doing.

Meanwhile, the Japanese economy was rising from the ashes of defeat, building new, modern plants. They were learning from American quality gurus like W. Edwards Deming and Joseph Juran that the road to success lies in paying attention to detail and turning out products upon which customers can rely. For decades, we looked the other way and refused to face up to what was happening and that it was happening because we had grown too bloated and complacent to think our ascendancy could ever be challenged.

Slowly, steadily, in industry after industry over the past decade we have gotten the wake-up call! As nations on the Pacific Rim and in the third world began to take customers and product markets one by one it became apparent that our best was no longer good enough. We began to pay attention to the theories (long ignored) of Deming, Juran, and others such as Philip Crosby, Armand Feigenbaum, and Kaoru Ishikawa. Concepts of total quality, continuous improvement, and zero defects became standard topics of discussion in board rooms and executive offices.[1]

A boom in the consulting industry resulted with a proliferation of "experts" ready to provide packaged programs to bring a company up to speed in what was becoming the hot new buzz word of business—Total Quality Management or "TQM".

Talking about this in the context of the world economy or even in terms of the nation or specific industries tends to miss the focus of what this is really about. Quality improvement is a battle which is fought in the trenches of individual companies as managements strive to bring about a turnaround in the way they and their people approach everyday tasks and repetitive encounters with customers. Though theories abound, it is certainly true that "quality" is in the eye of the beholder and determining how it will be manifested, identifying that "beholder", and determining how to get where the organization needs to be often is an imprecise science (though it is becoming more precise all the time as uniform quality standards are developed in various industries).

Just what is this thing called quality?

A story is told about five men who had never seen an elephant before being led into a totally dark room where one of the great beasts stood in the center. Each reached out and touched the animal and was asked to describe what an elephant was like. The first man, who had grabbed hold of the tail said, "An elephant is like a snake." The second, who held the trunk said, "It's like a firehose." The third, clinging to a leg, described it as similar to the trunk of a tree. A fourth, holding an ear said, "It's like a large palm leaf." The fifth man, who felt the elephant's side, said confidently, "An elephant is just like a wall!"

In a sense, quality is very similar to that elephant. How you perceive it depends on where you are standing and what part of it you've got your hands on!

At Brauer Supply in St. Louis we have been trying to get a hold on the elephant for some time now. Throughout industry at this time thousands of companies, large and small, are grappling after the same thing. Seeking a better handle on the beast so that it might be put to good use in the service of a profitable business, I commenced an extended series of discussions with CEO's, quality professionals, and specialty consultants around the country as part of a series written for *The Quality Observer, The International News Magazine of Quality*. I found very many differences in how people view the quality process and yet, there are many similarities. It is clear that business people are beginning to reach a consensus of where they want to be from a quality standpoint and they are finding various successful ways of getting there!

In the chapters that follow we'll join in a conversation with this network of the well-known and the not-so-well-known and look at the process of TQM as it is viewed today. We will examine the quality issues being debated in companies large and small. Hopefully, together, we can get a good grip on the elephant and put him to work for our businesses! ●●•

Reports From The Front Lines.

The Process

2

The Quality Policy—Getting It Down On Paper!

I t would be a rare company that didn't claim to deliver quality in at least one area—service, dependability, or precision of its products. Even competitive price could, in the eyes of some, be a component of quality value delivered.

The company intent on really doing something to make the quality concept a tangible reality will have to go beyond vague feelings of dedication and commitment and attempt to codify what it is the organization stands for, what it is trying to accomplish, what expectations it has for itself, and how it will judge success in its efforts. Thus it is that most corporate quality programs begin with the drafting of a written statement.

Putting a quality policy down on paper forces management or whoever is charged with the task to confront what it is that the company stands for as opposed to what it has traditionally said was its reason for being.

The benefits of putting the policy down in writing include clearly defining expectations for employees and providing a vehicle for communicating the program to the customer base. The policy can become a framework for all activities within the business. It can become the guiding rule to govern product development decisions, customer service activities, management decisions involving employee relations, and matters of corporate social responsibility. In effect it becomes a creed by which the organization and its employee members live.

With such long range and all-encompassing impact, the policy should not be hastily constructed , but should be a result of hours of soul searching by those who have the power to guide and direct the company. While it can be brief and direct in form, it does need to answer certain basic questions.

Companies often find themselves driven in different directions. Is the primary motivation to make a profit? Does the company exist for the benefit of the employees first? What about the customers—are they the primary focus of efforts?

The analytical process the policy drafters must go through takes a look at these diverse constituencies and sets the focus. When this process occurs, most companies will come to the conclusion that focusing on the customer eventually meets the needs of profits and employee welfare. The customer driven company, one that is obsessed with satisfying customers on a consistent basis, is very likely to be profitable. Employees will be an active part of the management process and feel greater satisfaction from their daily efforts.

The statement or "commitment to quality" should clearly set forth just what it is the company intends to do. It may assert that responding quickly and completely to all customer needs and maintaining business relationships based on honesty, trust, and mutual commitment are key goals. It may speak to such points as providing products in sufficient quantities at the correct time and place to meet customer needs or it may focus on accuracy and detail in transactions. Whatever it is the company intends to do, the policy should also set forth what the expected results of these intended actions will be.

The quality policy should be a shared statement of principles valued and used in achieving an organization's vision, says Thomas E. Good of 3M Quality Management Services. The Quality Management Services at 3M guides its clients through a strategic action sequence which includes training, education, planning, and project improvement. Under this program emphasis is on the importance of defining the company's mission first and then setting a five-year vision defining the direction in which the organization wants to go.

The objectives of this vision should be as follows:

1. *To show the direction and characteristics of the organization at a future point in time.*
2. *To position the customer's perception about the organization and the organization's image of itself.*

3. *To create a quality improvement plan to achieve a goal for each part of the organization.*

In line with this idea of "vision," companies focus on basic values which can serve as building blocks for growth. An example would be Boatmen's National Bank, the ten-state regional financial institution, where the quality policy takes the form of a four component commitment to quality, integrity, responsiveness, and efficiency.

Vice President Barbara Drago of Boatmen's says the written statement of values is widely disseminated to customers along with detailed data on statistical quality efforts and surveys to define customer needs and expectations. Extensive monthly "Quality Reports" are a key feature of the program for checking internal progress. Regular meetings of key department heads are held with the overriding concern of living up to the standards set forth in the statement.

At my own distribution company in St. Louis, we describe the actions we intend to take and then conclude by tying these together to the end result of serving as a valued partner in our customer's success. We further link this to opportunity for growth and personal satisfaction for our employees and suppliers which brings all three parties—customers, employees, and suppliers—into a common endeavor.

By speaking to these diverse elements, we hope to gain the support of all three in implementing our policy and insure that it will have staying power and not just be a brief effort at sloganeering.

The quality policy should be developed by consensus. It should have the backing of all department heads or key people and should be "sold" with vigor to employees at all levels. If it does not take into consideration the logical needs and viewpoints of employees at all levels the program runs the risk of being mocked by those who must carry it out.

Once the policy is developed, it is important to disseminate it as widely as possible. Employees must feel that the customer's eyes are on them to see if they will really deliver what is promised.

A mailing of the new policy explaining what it means should be made to all key customers. This puts the organization and its employees on the line—but that is a risk the company committed to quality must take. The statement can be printed up on high quality, engraved stationary, similar to a wedding invitation, or possibly engraved on some high quality memento such as marble paperweights or similar items. The idea is to ensure it will get the customer's attention. The policy should be prominently displayed at counter or customer contact areas where those receiving service can see the commitments the company and its employees are making.

Communicating the policy becomes a repetitive habit. New product developments, changes in procedures, expanded services—these can all be presented to customers as one more component of a comprehensive quality policy. The objective is to make the company name synonomous with "quality" in the minds of the target public.

With such a high visibility public standard, there is a great potential for embarrassment should service levels fall. It is just this potential, however, that can provide the extra motivation to insure that mistakes do not happen or, if they do, that the employees of the company react with great fervor to correct the situation.

In summary, the quality policy should be the result of intense self-examination by an organization's leaders to reflect where they want to go and for what they stand. It should speak of specific actions the company will undertake and the expected results to be achieved. Finally, it should stress the benefits to the diverse interest groups which are involved in the ultimate delivery of services to the customer. It should insure the customer is the focus and the driving force behind all efforts.

The successful quality policy sets forth a standard of performance which points toward one hundred per cent conformance to customer requirements. It is designed to build customer loyalty, employee morale, and to serve as the backbone on which a successful quality improvement process and a solid, long-term organization can be built. ●••

3

Role Of The Quality Steering Committee

Next to a committed management, the most important group in determining the success or failure of a quality program is the steering committee selected to oversee the process.

Oftentimes, especially in a small business, the whole program is initiated after the CEO or some key executive attends a quality seminar and comes back all fired up with the idea of implementing a program according to a specific format which has been laid out by some "expert". He is full of enthusiasm and is determined to communicate this to every single person in the company.

Typically, department heads are called in and the program is set before them. The managers give the appropriate obligatory response that, yes, they will do their best to get the program going. They then turn their attention to the day-to-day matters which are of more immediate concern. They may be wryly amused at the CEO's evangelical zeal for the concept.

"Of course we stand for quality," they say. "That's why we don't have time to mess with all this red tape!"

It is just that preoccupation with existing ways of doing things and avoidance of facing change that needs to be shaken to achieve the goal of product quality and service excellence. Those who will be expected to lead the charge must share the enthusiasm and dedication to looking at things in a new way if employees on down the line are to "buy in" to the concept.

Accordingly, it is most important that members of the Quality Steering Committee, who will constitute the apostles of change, must fully understand and be committed to the process. Ideally, they can also be participants in the outside quality training which has germinated the idea. In lieu of this, time must be spent away from daily interruptions to communicate and convey the sense of revolution which is inherent in a pervasive quality improvement program.

Should the steering committee be composed of department heads—or should it include a cross section of people from different levels of authority? There are arguments on both sides.

Including key managers and department chiefs ensures that employees will feel the stamp of approval from the top within their department and top management may be better able to control the content of the program. Also, these managers may be more likely to possess the administrative and communications skills to carry it off. On the other hand, if people from all levels of the work force are included in the committee, it may create more of a sense of ownership of the process by workers at all levels, may give the chance for a new "star" to shine, and may place responsibility on someone who makes membership on the steering group a primary focus of his or her activities.

At Indiana Supply in Indianapolis, Sales Manager Dave Draga heads up a steering committee which includes representation from six functional areas. These include administration, outside sales, inside sales, warehouse/plant, and the company's construction and commercial sectors. Representatives serve three year terms with one member being replaced every six months.

"We've been at this process for some five years," says Draga. "The steering committee's responsibility is to come up with things to keep interest focused on quality as a concept. We make sure quality is scheduled as a segment of each sales meeting and constantly develop exercises, teamwork projects, and resources for keeping quality at the forefront of everything we do."

In including someone from the work group, it is important that the individual be open to new ideas, have a strong sense of identity with the company, and a solid sense of self so that he or she is not afraid to stand up and endorse strange new concepts. For some people, asking them to assume a company leadership role may put them in an unfamiliar and uncomfortable position. It might be the equivalent of asking them to wear a "tutu" to work.

One manager I spoke with recalls when he initially started to form a steering committee at his distribution company and sought the participation of an employee who was an acknowledged leader amongst the warehouse workers. Initial efforts to entice this particular individual to join were unsuccessful. He obviously just would not feel comfortable standing up in his peer group championing a structured quality program. He was a dedicated worker, however, and once the program got under way he pitched right in!

Keeping this in mind, spots should be held open on the committee where key front line workers can be approached later after the program gets rolling and initial uneasiness is passed. In fact, gaining endorsement of the concept from an earlier skeptic may win over others who are holding back.

Once the committee is formed, they should have a hand in developing a written quality policy. Though top management will have certain concepts and guidelines in mind, the input from committee members will continue to give them ownershp and a stake in the process. Top management should be involved as chairman or a key player in this committee since commitment from the top will be the critical factor in the success or failure of the program.

Since quality is the goal, the operation of the committee itself must set a pattern. Meetings should start and end on time with a clearly stated purpose. Minutes should be kept and a list of action items developed.

The Indiana Supply steering committee meetings follow a structured plan. The once-a-month meetings are limited to one hour during which they move through old business, employee suggestion review, committee reports, selection of an employee of the month, and development of ad hoc project teams to address specific problems. A different committee member serves as moderator each month.

The whole quality process of setting goals and measuring their achievement should be mirrored in the committee's operation. There needs to be a firm agenda. Key managers should attend all meetings and measurements should be kept to see if they accomplish their assigned action items. They should practice quality methods in their committee functions and day-to-day responsibilities. Staff meetings at all levels should begin to incorporate the quality concept in everything undertaken.

Occasionally, it may be that someone on this committee does not fully buy into the concept and is not pulling his or her share of the load. If such is the case, he or she should be tactfully removed lest the program be undermined for others. If the program takes hold, membership on this group will become a high-status appointment and the commitment of these leaders will grow.

It is important that management delegate real authority to the steering committee. If ideas and plans are developed by consensus, the ability to implement them quickly is a visible manifestation of the employee empowerment lying at the heart of an effective TQ process.

Every successful movement, be it political, social, or cultural, stems from the efforts of a dedicated core group of individuals. This is certainly the case in quality implementation. Careful selection, training, and continued support of these people will ensure attainment of quality objectives by the entire company! ●•·

4

Setting Goals In The Quality Process

"**I**f you don't know where you're going any road will get you there!"

This often repeated saying is particularly applicable to the process of Total Quality Management.

Quality can be all things to all people. With several major schools of thought evolving and proponents of different methodologies vying for acceptance, the way is open for each company to shape and mold its own variation of a quality process. There is good and bad in this in that each company's customers, markets, and situation are unique and require tailored programs to meet specific needs—yet—the one constant faced by all enterprises is the existence of a customer base or constituency of some sort which has expectations and desires for the organization to fulfill.

Without targeting a destination there is danger that a company's TQM process can become nothing more than an ambiguous public relations program or an indirect attempt at building employee morale and pushing the workers for more output. Without a clear understanding of goals the company hopes to achieve by the quality process the whole undertaking can run out of steam after the initial hoopla has subsided. It is doubtless in recognition of this that specific target programs based on quality criteria such as Baldrige and ISO 9000 are sweeping through American industry. They provide a structure and a set of clearly defined targets which help to keep the quality efforts focused and on course.

Recognizing that customer satisfaction must be the ultimate barometer of a company's success, considerable attention must be centered on just what constitutes the customer's wants and needs. I address this in a later chapter ("The Quality Survey: Assessing Customer Needs"). But even after this is established there is a degree of latitude in determining which areas of improvement are to be emphasized and what specific results are to be sought. Companies approach these decisions in a variety of ways. Some view this as the rightful responsibility of senior management while others give considerably more weight to personnel trained in quality or the quality steering committee with feedback from front-line workers. Most utilize a combination of these to analyze customer needs and come up with initial goals.

At Mallinkrodt Medical, Inc. of St. Louis, a steering committee consisting of key director level personnel defines which programs are the most critical after which Quality Improvement Teams (QIT) are formed. These teams are trained in the Juran Quality Improvement Process with a trained leader and facilitator. The groups define problems and establish objectives and goals that are submitted to the quality steering committee for approval.

Scott Dickerhoff, senior product development engineer for the company's Anesthesiology Division, says that regular quality improvement team meetings are then held with status updates and project assignments, all geared toward pursuit of the defined goals. Quarterly steering committee meetings involve updates from the individual teams, discussing milestones achieved and how and when they were accomplished. "Milestones" are defined in a project plan with target dates. Reports of progress are published regularly.

Dickerhoff, a facilitator for one of Mallinkrodt's quality improvement teams, says, "Goals should be set so that they are attainable and so that gains along the way can be measured. They should be quantifiable and specific but not to the extent that they become constricting."

Overly broad or undefined goals can lead to a work group's frustration and result in ineffective action. This is the viewpoint of Robert Irwin, vice president of quality for Sverdrup Corporation, who comes down strongly on the side of goals that are numerical and quantifiable. Sverdrup is a full-service engineering, architectural, and construction company serving both the domestic and international market.

"We developed a strategic quality plan aimed at measurable improvement of specific work delivery processes," says Irwin. "The overall goals are decided by a quality committee composed of senior executives."

Sverdrup's approach to goal-setting in the quality process is to look at it from the customer's point of view. Within each work process there are sub-processes which impact upon the customer and specific improvement targets are set to serve as objectives. For example, design process may include processes for checking drawings, exceptions, reviewing vendor submittals, estimating, scheduling, and a number of other activities. Targets may include such things as reducing the percentage of checking and rework required which is non-value-added time for the clients.

Most of the focus at Sverdrup is on company-wide goals. Since individual managers are committed to bettering these company standards, they naturally identify problem areas and develop individual goals for their resolution.

Proponents of TQM are apt to describe their ultimate goal as one hundred per cent defect-free products or services. The theory is that to accept anything less is to express a tolerance for failure (even to a minor degree) which is conceptually inconsistent with the total quality mindset. But is the targeting of such a goal so unrealistic as to discourage employees from buying into the quality concept because they feel the end goal is unrealistic and unattainable?

Irwin feels that while one hundred per cent defect-free work may (emphasis on "may") never be achieved, it still is a worthy goal. Dickerhoff, on the other hand, believes that such a standard is unrealistic, arguing that each product or service must be evaluated and targets established that are attainable. They should be ones that can be maintained to hold any gains.

Who decides when goals have been achieved and by what criteria? Certainly top management must take a hand in this and monitor results, providing for appropriate recognition for outstanding performance. The system of "milestones" instituted at Mallinkrodt has been outlined above and this is similar to procedures at many large companies. A small business, on the other hand, is far more likely to have success or failure judged subjectively by top management involved to an intimate degree with daily operations.

Once achieved, do the goals remain the same or are new goals set?

"Basic goals remain constant," says Sverdrup's Irwin, "but annual goals may be revised when improvement is necessary."

As companies and their quality teams delve more and more deeply into the quality process new problems are uncovered and areas of weakness defined. This then leads to new problem definitions and setting of goals to remedy situations.

Part and parcel of the quality process is the idea of hundreds of individual workers working diligently to improve similar hundreds of small processes, procedures, and product components. This inherently involves goal setting on an individual level whether established by the employee him- or herself or by a supervisor or quality team. More often than not the employee is guided in this goal selection by authority established by the company.

Says Mallinkrodt's Dickerhoff, "All employees should set short and long term career goals though many do not. These personal career goals are quite different from company goals but workers need to realize that if they help to meet company goals it will be much easier to reach individual career goals."

Given the centrality of goals and their attainment to the quality process, as well as the motivating force they can provide, it is important that workers are regularly and consistently advised of progress. Knowledge that the company and its employees are successfully chipping away at objectives can improve morale and spur people to greater efforts. Conversely, workers kept in the dark begin to suspect that quality efforts are a meaningless waste of time which, for all they know, may merely be adding to cost and thereby diminishing profit without tangible result.

Goal setting should be an evolving process and should employ all the tools available to supply accurate and meaningful information. The changes and improvement will not occur overnight. It will require a great deal of time and hard work. This is not something you do in your spare time!

The commitment must come from the top down and it must be clear that the goals are indeed quality related, not sales or production quotas.

A science or an art? Perhaps there is a little of both. Here we look for a specificity that lends itself to measurement, but the choice of direction and what we ultimately want to achieve touches upon our aspirations and indeed our faith in ourselves. The skill of the engineer is needed, but the vision of the dreamer has its role here also. ●●•

5

The Quality Consultant

Setting out on the road to quality means "getting outside the box" of traditional methods and procedures. Both workers and management must be ready to discard the mental approach they may have been using for years. This is not always easy and not always bloodless.

Gaining acceptance for a new way of thinking is made easier if it is a concept introduced by someone from the outside who brings a fresh perspective and whose recommendations are backed up by successful experience at other companies and in other industries.

Thus it is that most companies utilize the services of a "consultant" in some form. This may be an expert who comes in and works individually with company management and who works on premise or it may be the leader of a training seminar attended by management and a proposed quality steering committee. How far an organization goes in utilizing this consultant's services may depend upon the company's size, resources, and the depth of the problems it is trying to correct or the scope of the change it is trying to effect.

"The consultant provides a good sounding board for development of ideas," says President Russ Broeckelmann of Coastline Distribution, Inc. in Sanford, Florida. "He provides a resource to help keep the project going. The company has made an investment by paying him and he sets appointments, schedules, and keeps things on course."

Broeckelmann has the unique advantage of having worked on both sides of the consulting table. He was for many years CEO of Houston's Thermal Supply Company before founding the consultant firm Precision Distribution Systems. Recently he was called on to head up the large network of Coastline branches throughout the Southeast.

At Indiana Supply in Indianapolis, President Stan Hurt is a strong advocate of utilizing the outside expert.

"People inside a company are too close to see what they're doing wrong," says Hurt. "It helps to get the perspective of different people and companies which a consultant can provide. Sometimes people are willing to say things with a consultant in the room that they might not otherwise say."

Hurt's company began the process with attendance by key managers at a seminar which sparked interest in the quality process and then, as efforts began to unfold, he brought in two outside advisors, each with a slightly different focus on components of the quality process.

"The outside expert can kick everyone into high gear," says Hurt. "The consultants we chose made us goal oriented. We had goals established in our various departments, but they helped us tie all of them into a coherent set of company goals."

Consultant Don Kardux of Business Navigators in Toledo, Ohio, says the consultant can bring the benefits of time and experience. He can compress the time needed to reach decisions and get the process going. This can mean a less expensive start-up and faster pay back.

While people know what to do, when they have to develop the process from scratch it will take too long.

Kardux developed his theories over many years while working with Lennox Industries in their "Dealer Marketing Advisor" program. As part of this he conducted extensive workshops, guiding groups of small contractors through an analysis of their total business.

In selecting a consultant, most business people I spoke with stress again the need for choosing someone with hands-on experience with companies in the TQ process. This seems to take precedence over formal educational or organizational credentials. It is helpful if he or she has a knowledge of a company's specific industry, but that is not of paramount importance. In fact, sometimes whole industries need an infusion of fresh ideas and someone from outside of the industry can bring that new viewpoint.

Kardux divides consultants into two groups. One group provides "knowledge".

"This is like a CPA or computer expert,"he says. " They'll teach you how to do a particular system they know in detail. When you know what you want to achieve, this kind of person can serve you well."

The other group focuses on teaching a process and is the consultant-type most often encountered in TQM. This consultant teaches how to set up procedures and change actions that lead to quality. Kardux likens this to the old saying that, "People are better served if we teach them how to fish rather than give them a fish."

It is important to understand a consultant's over-all philosophy. Listen carefully in your initial discussions with the advisor to see if his ideas are consistent with those of management.

"The quality philosophy is about making people accountable for performing their mission right the first time," says Hurt. "If the consultant can help people achieve that it will benefit both the company and its customers."

How should the consultant's services be delivered? Should he or she be physically on site at the company?

At Indiana Supply, the advisor spent several days with management preparing for meetings with employees. Following this there were numerous phone calls and information flowing back and forth. The consultant spent an equal amount of time researching and making group presentations.

Quality Coach Cay Bradley of IBM's Wholesale Distribution Group says the outsider's focus should be on providing training to the people who will serve as leaders within the company. Trained leaders should then go and teach the line workers.

Bradley became involved with IBM's quality program after years of experience as a sales rep and marketing manager working with large customers who were among the first to focus on statistical process control. She also began to teach classes for IBM employees designed to center on the company culture, quality, and change. She teaches about process improvement and leads process teams. This helps her see the importance of developing quality group leaders.

Kardux agrees that training the trainers is of first importance.

At companies where he helps in setting up TQM he follows up by coming in once a month for a year. After that, if the management has a handle on the process, Kardux feels they should be able to take it and run with it.

"You need to teach the process and let them do it—then just get out!" he says.

Should the consultant be a quality specialist or can he or she focus on more than just quality topics? Most of those surveyed seem to feel that a good over-all perspective on business functions along with an understanding of TQM principles is important. Therefore, it is not necessarily a prerequisite that the consultant specialize in quality unless a specific format (such as ISO 9000) is targetd.

"If you're going to hire someone to help you implement quality he or she should have a strong understanding of the criteria to be used," says Broeckelmann.

"Quality reaches into every single aspect of everything we do," says Kardux. "You can't just focus on quality and leave the accounting alone. Quality is a filter through which every part of the company must pass."

Should the consultant be exclusive to the company he serves within its market? This is probably irrelevant, though many companies may require it as part of their initial contract with the advisor. Some in industry view the whole quality process as a concept that must be shared and see it as raising the level of entire industries.

"Quality is so personal and different that two companies in the same market probably wouldn't interfere with each other's programs," says Broeckelmann. "At each company it takes on a personality of its own. To some, quality is very motivational, but to me it's people dealing with people on a golden rule basis. It's partnering all the way down the line. We must ask—because we don't know—what's in the mind of the consumer?"

"The more competitors viewing their business from a quality perspective, the more profitable a market will be," says Hurt. "A high tide raises all ships."

In evaluating the outside advisor, perhaps the most important factor is his or her list of satisfied customers. Talk to those who have used the person's services and find out how he or she relates to the people and what positive changes have resulted in the organization.

How should the consultant be compensated? It may be in the form of a set fee or a percentage of bottom line improvement or improvement in specific process measurements. The latter is difficult to quantify on a meaningful level and could have the effect of skewing the consultant's recommendations toward short-term improvements. Therefore, most users and consultants opt for a fixed fee.

"Paying by percentage leaves too many things open to interpretions," says Broeckelmann. "A percentage of what? Too many factors can be argued about, all of which detract from the quality focus."

"With a set fee both parties know where they stand," says Kardux. "There is no concern about objectivity of advice. Having a fixed fee is the safest way to protect against this kind of temptation."

Hurt agrees that the fee makes things simpler for everyone. He cites the difficulty in coming up with a meaningful percentage measurement which would not be subject to question when the final numbers are compiled.

Of course, hiring a consultant, going through the exercises, and then ignoring the advice can kill the momentum of a quality program. Therefore, it's vitally important that management has previewed the philosophy of the individual sufficiently that they know in which direction the consultant will head with his or her program and whether or not they will be able to enthusiastically concur in the recommendations. One has to be careful, of course, that this does not limit the open communication that needs to develop. It may well be that a complete turnabout from current methods will be necessary. By this I mean only that management does not want to be "surprised" by the basic philosophy and orientation of their chosen advisor.

Talk to previous customers, visit with the consultant, and listen carefully to how he or she plans to approach your organization.

If a good match is found, the outsider can get things going quickly and have you moving down the quality trail following a tried and true roadmap! ●••

6

The Quality Survey: Assessing Customer Needs

The mail department brought in a stack of postage-paid reply envelopes and dropped them on my desk. I picked up a couple of pieces and eagerly tore them open to read the responses our customers were making to the survey we had developed at the commencement of our quality program. The first one I read made me stop short and shake my head at the realization of an obvious blunder.

"The survey form doesn't fit into the envelope. End of survey!" wrote the customer.

He was right. In my haste to get the program going in my distribution business I had utilized some small postage-paid envelopes I had on hand while the survey form we had developed folded to fit into a standard #10 envelope. It was hardly the "quality" image we hoped to convey.

In the first load of customer replies I had learned a valuable lesson about viewing things from the customer/recipient point of view. It was to be one of many that were gleaned from the effort and helped to shape the objectives and methods of our infant quality program.

Indeed, quality programs seem to flounder most frequently when efforts are rigidly developed according to a pre-packaged formula and are not specifically tied to customer needs. Recognizing this, there is an increasing effort to design programs to respond to those things the customer values most. Many businesses are reviewing their sales commissions and managerial bonuses to tie them directly to customer satisfaction and retention.

How do we find out what is important to the customer? On the surface that seems to be the job of the sales force, and a well-trained team of representatives can help keep a company clued in and focused on customer objectives. But even the most perceptive representative can see things through rose-colored glasses or be the victim of his or her own defensiveness or biases.

It is for this reason that formalized surveys before and during a quality implementation are integral parts of such programs. In reaching out in this way, the customers become partners in setting standards of service and guiding allocation of company resources.

The survey of current customer satisfaction levels is a good jumping off point for the commencement of a quality program. Not only does it point out the strengths and weaknesses of an organization and provide a base from which to measure improvements resulting from quality efforts, but it also sends a clear message to customers that their views are important and will play a part in the molding of services to be offered by the company.

The sophistication of the initial survey can vary depending on the size of the company and the resources available. Larger organizations may have their own market research people who are skilled at designing such questionaires. An organization of any size can hire outside professionals to get the job done or a small business owner can develop his own survey, recognizing that it may reflect some of his own biases and beliefs. The goal, of course, is to gain an objective snapshot of the business and its services as its customers see it.

Why is it important to determine customer satisfaction levels?

"Meeting customer needs is how companies will distinguish themselves from each other in the 1990's," says Janet Varner who is senior project manager for research at Boatmen's Bancshares. "In the absence of this, services become mere commodities."

At Boatmen's Bancshares, the midwestern bank holding company, surveys of the customer base are a regularly scheduled procedure and form an integral part of an ongoing Total Quality process.

Varner said Boatmen's initiated an extensive survey at the outset of its quality program and followed up with annual surveys. Most of the questions on the form remain the same for tracking purposes but new topics are introduced as needed. The initial twelve page questionaire, which was sent by mail, was returned with a twenty-five percent return rate from corporate customers and an astonishing forty percent from retail bank customers.

Response to the retail form was encouraged by use of a one dollar incentive payment included with the form. Every effort was made to project a professional image with the survey and to make it clear that customer opinions are valued highly.

The Boatmen's survey contained a mix of multiple choice, objective questions, and an open area for comments. Following a pattern often seen in such questionaires, the majority of respondents chose not to fill in anything in this comment area. Mail responses were verified by significant phone sampling using a shortened version of the survey. The surveys generally are quite comprehensive and customers of competitors are also surveyed to compile normative data.

Research of this type often results in few surprises, but serves to verify or reinforce the company's pre-existing perceptions of its own strengths and weaknesses. Those developing the format need to be aware of a tendency to support these expectations and must ensure that questions are objective and non-biased. Customers are free to return the surveys without signing their names though they may elect to identify themselves. This option is one of the basic ethical guidelines applied to this kind of market research.

A great deal of time and energy can be devoted to the customer survey, but all too frequently the survey becomes an end in itself and the information obtained is put to little use. The real trick is in translating it into specific actions to improve the company's performance. At United Van Lines, the world-wide moving company, the interpretation and practical application of data derived from customer surveys is the focal point of the company's Total Quality program, says John Hohenstein. Hohenstein is part of a twenty-five member task force in the home office, each member of which is assigned from six to eight United Van Lines agents (similar to franchisees) in different locales to assist in reviewing customer survey responses and working on methods and procedures to meet the expressed customer needs and expectations. Task force members each must complete a twenty-one hour training session under the tutelage of United's Organizational Development Director Mike Dace.

Every shipper who utilizes United Van Lines is mailed an extensive multi-page questionaire with the opportunity to rate service and responsiveness numerically. The different components of the company's service are broken down into units for evaluation including the sales process, estimating, van operators, packers, loaders, and over-all communication with the customer. In addition to numerical ratings, space is provided for written comments.

The key question the company focuses on, according to Hohenstein, is "What kind of efforts or services will it take for you to use or recommend United Van Lines?" It is these responses that guide the company and its agents in molding methods and procedures.

Hohenstein reports a forty percent response rate returning the questionaires, which can be returned anonymously if the customer so desires. Results are sent to agents on a quarterly basis. Each member of the task force has a composite of the responses affecting his assigned agent and helps interpret the scores and counsels the principal of the agent company. In addition to sharing survey data, an active customer service department directly monitors customer complaints and suggestions.

The program in its present format has been in operation for one year with a "one hundred percent commitment to the future," says Hohenstein.

The survey was developed with outside professional assistance as well as in-house expertise. The outside help ensured that the questions were presented in an unbiased manner, free from preconceived ideas or expectations.

There was some apprehension among the agents when the program was instituted, according to Hohenstein, but this has had the effect of heightening awareness of customer service issues. Many agents were surprised by the survey results, discovering strengths and weaknesses of which they were unaware, or learning that customer concerns focused on issues to which they had not attributed much importance.

"One of our slogans is 'Quality shows in every move we make,'" says Hohenstein. "Quality and service go hand in hand and we intend to raise our service levels up to customer expectations."

Since customers over-all may have a tendency to be overly kind in their responses, it is important that the work force not become complacent after receiving a preponderance of positive comments. This is one instance where the concept of "zero defects" should be applied. Any negative comments or ratings, no matter how small statistically, should be cause for concern and attention. Areas of weakness highlighted by the survey should be analyzed and suggestions for improvement developed by "action groups" of employees.

Should survey results be open to inspection by employees and the public? Views vary on this since publishing results can give competitors information with which they might exploit weaknesses or gain insight into a company's strategy. Certainly the fullest internal communication of the results and the meaning to worker groups must be undertaken. Some companies break the data into small components, giving each department only the information affecting that particular unit.

The large public companies, accustomed to the spotlight of publicity, often publish their results and state their plans to meet the needs expressed. While small privately-held businesses guard their privacy jealously, more and more they are opening up as they begin to perceive customers as partners and the quality process becomes more of an integral part of their operations.

At Brauer Supply in St. Louis, we made it a point to send a letter of thanks to each customer who returned a survey and chose to sign his or her name. Where specific deficiencies were noted, top management of the company either spoke directly with a concerned customer or a sales representative carried information about our plans to deal with the problem.

It is this two-way communication which the quality survey provides that channels and directs TQ efforts. This communication is a starting point—and an end in itself— for successful implementation. ●●•

7

Employee Teams And The Quality Process

Quality starts with the individual—with one person's dedication to a defect-free, excellent product or service. The company provides a supportive environment by establishing a quality culture. One of the most effective methods of bringing about this culture and helping individuals strive for quality, however, is by the use of groups or "teams" to develop structures, devise new procedures, and attack problems.

The use of teams, whether they are designated as "quality circles," "action groups," "self-managed teams," or "task forces," is invariably a critical component of successful quality programs. The pooling of individual resources and ideas into a group provides reinforcement and encourages further development of concepts. Peer pressure and responsibility to co-workers can help encourage individuals to make the maximum contribution to the quality process and fosters a sense of "ownership" of the quality program.

Whose responsibility is it to provide the structure for quality teams and to provide the direction?

"It is management's prerogative," says Jim Widtfeldt of Honeywell. "That's how you get things started, but much of this will become self-generating. Management can affirm the whole process but should establish criteria and help set priorities."

Widtfeldt, a fourteen year Honeywell employee, is currently manager of quality education at Honeywell's Home and Building Controls organization in Golden Valley, Minnesota, where he conducts employee surveys, does team building, promotes organizational development, and creates communication packages to continue to build the organization's quality culture. Widtfeldt does quality improvement consulting for other divisions of Honeywell, and many refer to him as a "culture engineer."

Between 1985 and 1987 Widtfeldt was co-founder and associate director of quality concepts for a Honeywell venture called Quality Management Systems which was a profit center offering experience-based training and consulting services to other companies. The venture was reabsorbed into the corporation during recent restructuring.

"The reason quality circles were so popular in their heyday was that they provided appropriate structures for identifying and solving problems," says Widtfeldt. "The problem is that managers never saw them as integral to the business. They were viewed as something to keep the workers happy, but the real work and decisions went on in the carpeted office."

It's management's nature, says Widtfeldt, to resist letting go and handing over some of the authority to employee teams. When this resistance is present the company can miss out on the good things that can naturally flow from effective teams.

Benefits of approaching the quality process through teams include greater sharing of ideas, building upon the complementary skills of others, a heightened sense of community, more open communication, and increased motivation. The team concept can help to break down walls which exist between management/supervisory and line workers and between union and non-union employees.

Let's take a look at "team" efforts under way now at some companies considered leaders in their industries, and see how management is integrating the concept into their Total Quality programs.

● Quality Teams at United Parcel Service

United Parcel Service, the national package delivery company, has established a reputation for on-time service and quick response to customer needs. Involvement of their line workers is a key part of the company's success and, to this end, they have established a program known as KORE which stands for "Keeping Our Reputation For Excellence".

Focusing on involvement of hourly line workers in customer service, problem-solving, and continual improvement, the program was developed a number of years ago with strong management backing and is now under the direction of National Coordinator Al Renzenbrink.

United Parcel's Missouri District Customer Service Manager Stan Jones describes the program as a voluntary series of committees within the working departments designed to create awareness and a good "working together" attitude. It is intended to help people feel that they are a part of the decision-making process.

KORE committees are composed of groups of four to eight workers with one management or supervisory member. A chairman is selected from the line workers to serve as coordinator and the group tries to identify and correct service problems or devise means of improving operations. An annual theme is selected for the KORE groups which serves as a general focus, but subsidiary goals are often developed and specific problems attacked.

While the committees have been in existence for seven years, membership has shifted from year to year as new volunteers have sought to participate and others have completed their contributions. Jones estimated that approximately five percent of United Parcel employees are involved on the KORE committees at any one time, yet they serve as a conduit of communication to the entire employee base.

"Throughout United Parcel," said Jones, "our 260,000 people are involved in maintaining our reputation for excellent service so that we can continue to be a leader in the package distribution service industry."

● "QUALITY ALLIANCE" at Color Art

Teams of six to eight employees across the spectrum of responsibility spearhead problem solving and help find ways to meet and exceed customer expectations at Color Art, Inc., says Joseph Steiner, president of the Office Interiors Division of the midwest distributor of office furniture.

Color Art has developed a process called "Quality Alliance" in conjunction with manufacturer Steelcase, Inc., whose products the company sells. As part of this a designated over-all quality administrator devotes his full attention to the success of the program and serves as ex-officio member of all groups.

Problems are outlined through customer interviews after which a team develops a mission statement and a plan for resolving the situation. This is then reviewed and approved by management. Eventually, all of the company employees become involved in teams. While initial participation is voluntary, attempts are made to ensure all employees will have input. The "cross-functional" nature of the groups is key, with representation

31

from management, supervison, and line/mission workers on each team.

While some groups (such as a recognition and reward committee) have perpetual lives, most are developed to attack a single problem and cease to exist when the goal is achieved. The committees generally focus on a single issue, but the long-standing groups may be multifaceted.

What has been the result of the Color Art quality process?

"We receive comments from our customers all the time that tell us there has been improvement in our customer service levels and product quality," says Steiner. "In addition, we do surveys twice a year of our customer base to tell us if there has been a change in our customers' perception of the job we are doing."

While they have not yet included customers or suppliers on the committees, the company is considering "advisory groups" of these outside parties to help in defining expectations in the entire chain of product delivery.

Examples of specific problems that have been remedied by committee action include such things as the development of a customer notification program for errors, omissions, or damaged goods, and a reduction in what they term "inherited inventory." This is material returned to Color Art because of damage, mistakes, or similar occurrences.

As the quality process has evolved across the country, the concept of teams has progressed from the original focus on "quality circles" to teams that are more self-managed and which have more authority to determine objectives and evaluate individual efforts.

Steiner points to the basic difficulty of scheduling time for groups of workers from different departments to get together to devote uninterrupted attention to a problem. Other problems which could be encountered include the tendency of management to view committees as an easy hand-off of a problem rather than making the necessary tough decisions. Committees can also take off on a tangent and depart from management's objectives.

If committees are perceived as having real authority, then membership could become a high-status position and people could see it as a stepping-stone to greater responsibility.

Within the quality movement itself, recognition is developing for the roles small teams can play in implementing the process. While most national quality awards are directed to companies, the Rochester Institute of Technology, in combination with USA Today, has established a "Quality Cup" competition for teams and individuals who make significant contributions to the improvement of products and/or services in an organization. In recent years, hundreds of individuals and teams have been nominated for their front-line efforts to improve quality. Five national winners are awarded the Cup annually.[1]

Clearly, teams of workers pulling together to solve problems and reach company objectives can and should be a vital component of any successful quality program. The company which succeeds in putting together networks of these small groups will be building structures and teaching skills that will become a permanent part of the culture. ●●•

8

Serving The Internal Customer

One of the unique features of structured Total Quality programs is the recognition that we have "customers" throughout our organization whose expectations must be met.

In so many organizations, the vast majority of workers are far removed from the ultimate consumer and it becomes very easy to forget that all of our actions impact on whether or not that customer makes the decision to purchase our goods or services. When a company is involved in TQM all employees are taught to realize the importance of meeting expectations all the way down the chain to that ultimate customer.

This is one of the most easily understood concepts of the quality process. If there is to be an immediate change in customer service levels within an organization, this will provide employees with a tangible exercise which they can readily apply.

"You can see the light bulb go on when we introduce the idea of 'internal customers', " says Parker-Kalon's Jo Ellen Lemmon. "Some of the more intangible concepts take a long time to sink in, but people can readily understand this relationship."

Lemmon, quality assurance supervisor at this division of Black & Decker, is responsible for Parker-Kalon quality with respect to customer contact, outside vendors, inspections, accreditations, and customer surveys. Like many quality managers, her position evolved from previous responsibilities as leader of project teams. In her case she had led the implementation of MIS software for statistical process control.

"We all know how to treat an external customer," says President Pat Geary of Geary Pacific Corporation in Anaheim, California, "but we have to teach employees to think in terms of internal customers. We have to help them see that a customer is anyone whose cooperation you need to get your job done."

Geary, former president of the Northamerican Heating, Refrigeration and Air Conditioning Wholesalers Association, says employees must learn how to seek cooperation of internal customers. We are all interdependent, he says, and if the delivery person doesn't deliver in a timely manner or if accounting doesn't properly prepare invoices, then the whole thing can blow up in our faces. Management sets the tone by constantly advocating team efforts. This is like the coordinated style of a football team rather than the individualism of a baseball player.

"It's everybody's job to protect the quarterback," says Geary.

At Brauer Supply Company, the focus on serving internal customers was the centerpiece of activities in the first days of our quality effort. Members of the steering committee met with every employee and determined in each case who were the customers, both external and internal, of the given worker.

Once the internal customers were identified, one was selected by each employee for an initial thirty day exercise and that individual was brought into a conference with a steering committee member to talk about his or her expectations. The employee was then led through a discussion of the cost of not meeting the expectations and, alternatively, the benefits that would flow from meeting those requirements. A plan was developed to improve the specific effort, along with agreement on how improvement would be measured and when we would know if the goal had been achieved.

Following the session a memo was sent by the committee member/ facilitator to both the employee and his or her internal customer reviewing what had been agreed upon and stating that a progress check would be made midway through the month. At that point a brief joint meeting was held to see if procedures were being followed. Adjustments were made as necessary. At the end of the thirty day period the internal customer gave his assessment of the progress backed up by as many specific measurements as the trio had been able to identify. The meeting process then repeated itself with new internal customers selected or a continuation with the old if work was still needed on the requirements.

The reactions of employees vary but, for the most part, people will make a good effort because for the first time their work has a delivery point where a receiver of their efforts will stand in review.

How do we encourage internal customers to clearly state their needs and give feedback when these needs are not met? That is dependent partly on the skill of the steering committee member or the facilitator who guides the employees through these meetings.

"It's one-on-one conversations that bring out these needs," says IBM Quality Coach Cay Bradley. "We try to focus on what's wrong and 'How can I help you?' It could be as simple as a one-time fix."

Parker-Kalon's Lemmon says the concept of internal customers helps to bring problems that have long been submerged to the surface. Sometimes small problems become mountains, however, when people begin to perceive themselves as customers.

"It is important to define what are the critical needs on which to focus," says Lemmon. "The facilitator must help people evaluate this and find a happy medium."

Since internal customers invariably cross department lines, inter-department jealousies can arise which can block communication. How can these be surmounted? Again, it comes down to one-on-one human relationships within a framework which focuses on problems, not personalities. The whole message of the Total Quality program must hammer away at the idea that all employees exist in a partnership to create a smoother running, more profitable company.

"Try to let the employees know that all departments are interrelated," says Jeff Holmes, who is quality assurance manager at Airguard Industries in Louisville, Kentucky. "If one department needs a particular item others must remember that they will eventually be requiring things from other areas. They need to treat the requesting department as they would like to be treated."

Holmes, like Lemmon, had a background in computer science which he supplemented with line experience as a production supervisor at the company which identifies itself as "the complete source for air filtration products." When problems were experienced with a new product line, management expressed interest in developing a specialist in the quality area. Filling that slot, Holmes reports to the vice president of operations and monitors ingoing and outgoing goods, work in progress, and sets up controls.

At Airguard the plant supervisors meet together every morning with the plant manager to talk about things coming up and what they will need from other departments. This may include such things as a loaned employee, solving problems with raw materials, or other needs.

The process of social equalization that often comes as an outgrowth of TQM can help to remedy ego-related problems.

If one department is staffed by a group of degreed professionals, for example, they may be accustomed to ignoring valid comments and suggestions from a clerical group processing statements or people on the customer service desk. By forcing a highly compensated and highly educated group to view other groups of workers as "customers" it starts to break down barriers and insures that the front-line experience of the lower level workers is taken seriously when recommendations and suggestions are brought forward.

Most employees could select multiple internal customers served by their job. Working on detailed improvement for all of them at one time might overwhelm a person and burn out his or her desire to effectively participate in a quality improvement process. Sometimes, too, there is a tendency to pick the most urgent problem for a focus, though it may not be the most significant.

"We try to look at which internal efforts will serve outside customers," says Lemmon. "What can we do for people and departments within the company to enhance service to the ultimate purchasers?"

This can lead to a focus on relationships and procedures whereby costs can be reduced and production runs more smoothly, all affecting the delivery of services to the external customer.

Are there situations where the internal parties don't really want to resolve problems? Do they view the busy work of dealing with the problems as job security? How does management resolve this?

"You've got to get the parties together," says Geary. "Identify the problem and point out the positive effects to the company and the workers themselves of solving it. Again, stress the team concept."

IBM devoted major efforts to coming up with solutions to eliminate unneeded work. Recognition was given when an idea cut costs or removed redundant work.

"Management must be sensitive to employee concerns for security," says Bradley, "and stress the positive effects to the company and its growth from working more efficiently."

It is important that management demonstrate that no one gets in trouble if a correction is made on the front side of a problem. If a trend can be spotted, corrections can be made and things fixed before much harm is done. The idea is to avoid patching or band-aiding. Show them the benefits of cost saving and improvement and how it can keep the customers buying and therefore make things better for everyone.

How does management monitor progress on serving internal customers?

Bradley says that in IBM's Wholesale Distribution Industry Group, specific managers "own" each process team. While employees meet regularly to work through the process, the manager takes responsibility to ensure its implementation.

Parker-Kalon posts service levels everywhere throughout their office and plant in Campbellsville, Kentucky. This includes such measures as "ship-completes," defective and damage-free product, and safety records. Considerable emphasis is put on charting performance and this keeps the results right out in front of all employees.

At Airguard, management receives a monthly report which details progress on meeting the needs of internal customers via certain key measurements.

Relating to an internal customer allows every employee of an enterprise to be on the "front lines." It drives home the importance of customer service and makes clear the reason for their jobs' existence. As a starting point for Total Quality, it's a relatively simple exercise which can be repeated with regularity with tangible results. ●••

9

Employee Empowerment And The Quality Process

"**E**mpowerment of employees"—a catch phrase of the 1990's which, in many people's minds, has become synonomous with the quality movement.

Driven by worker teams from the shop floor to the policy level, TQM balances on twin premises of total customer satisfaction and reliance on front-line personnel to analyze, diagnose, recommend, and implement remedies to all problems. It is based on the supposition that front-line workers are first to see and feel the impact of poor service on product quality.

This "empowering" of employees to initiate change often comes within the context of specific quality procedures and guidelines which set parameters for decision-making. Sometimes it is these procedures which, if too zealously applied, actually hamstring employee flexibility. Without proper orientation the program may seem constricting rather than liberating from the perspective of the average employee.

Former vice president of human resources and community relations for Nestle, USA, Powell Woods says, "Employee empowerment is the heart and soul of a quality program, but it's not something that is easily achieved."

Production employees often see so many newfangled programs come and go that they find it very difficult to take them seriously. Hence, they will tend to "posture" acceptance of new programs, but feel very little real commitment toward them.

While not deliberately sabotaging or ignoring quality programs, line employees may tend not to "go the extra mile" to make them work and, of course, that is exactly what is needed to make them work! The result of this is that the implementation of true continuous quality improvement, with responsible statistical assessment, feedback, and production technique improvement, is a long, arduous, expensive, and laborious process.

Employees may tend to miss the basic thrust of the program, which is that they now have a say in the operation of their company, and focus instead on the required meetings and procedures necessary to bring this about. This reluctance means that there may be a long success curve with patience required for eventual payback. Management must be willing to settle for, and defend, lower margins than might otherwise be achievable for several years in order to deliver a better product five or ten years down the road. This is very difficult in the "instant gratification" American business culture.

In addition to failures of employee perception and management patience, other dangers lurk in instant empowerment without a well-planned stucture. These include:

1. *Workers may not consider the whole picture beyond their own activities. An example might be a forklift driver who has to fill his own propane tank. He may see a cost saving in time if filled tanks are brought in from the outside. He may never ask what the cost of this is to the company.*

2. *Empowerment cannot be total. Is an employee to be allowed to shut down a machine or line if he sees a small quality defect? Is this always justified in pursuit of total quality or is there a limitation where the cost far outweighs the significance of the quality deviation? What sanctions are there for a grossly bad judgement in the name of quality?*

3. *Executive follow-through may be lacking. If a program is set into motion it still needs direction and the ultimate measurement is still the bottom line of the company. If people are set free but are given no guidance on how to channel their new empowerment then people will be doing their own thing in their own area and it will be a challenge to bring costs back into line.*

Keith Dierberg, instructor in management at Concordia University of Mequon, Wisconsin, cautions that employees don't necessarily look at the cost of quality. This is something which is management's responsibility.

"It's important that management communicates boundaries in which quality must occur. Productivity can't be decreased. Overtime shouldn't increase. It is management's job to define boundaries of the playing field...the lower level can call the plays if management sets the rules of the game."

By constantly focusing on customer needs, the internal needs of an organization and its employees can sometimes take a backseat. Is this then a form of disempowering of workers in preference to the wishes of customers?

Dierberg, whose management background is derived from his experience in the retail grocery industry, disagrees. He says the customer's needs become a target and employees are given a degree of autonomy in defining the means of delivering a quality product. Under TQM this is formulated from the lowest level and works its way back up.

The disempowering aspects of quality programs were shared with me by an executive of a major midwestern company where the quality process had fallen on difficult times.

"Management must take hold and become responsible for quality and not totally abandon it to employees," he says. "It must be remembered that there is still work to perform and this cannot stop while meeting after meeting and daily experiments are going on."

There may be reluctance on the part of some employees to accept their newly broadened responsibility. If all policies are completely redefined it may frighten these workers and some truly do not want to participate in decision making.

Dierberg stresses the difference between job enrichment and job enlargement. Are employees given more input and more autonomy or is work just added to the person's normal load? Job enrichment is more vertical—the giving of authority. Job enlargement is a horizontal action which seems to the worker to be just piling on more duties and which may be greeted with suspicion.

Labor unions, too, may approach this new worker empowerment cautiously. By the very nature of TQM, unions are forced to look at the work force and their jobs in a different manner. Concepts of job shifting, job rotations, and changing to other tasks are foreign to traditonal labor union thinking. The concept that everyone is concerned with all aspects of quality runs counter to the traditional "this is my job" way of looking at specific assignments.

Why should a union participate? At the most basic level it is about preservation of jobs. With global competition and new companies constantly starting up, the union must realize it has to adapt to change or its membership will decrease. Their success hinges on the success of the organization.

Woods tells about what he describes as one of the greatest success stories in quality assurance and improvement which occurred at Stouffer Foods. This Nestle operating company lost money every quarter in the early 1960's until they achieved a reputation for having the finest frozen food product in the marketplace. They spared no cost, buying only the finest ingredients and fine-tuning the recipes until they got them just right. They convinced their employees that they were serious about quality, ultimately showing them that success in the marketplace was achievable through developing and maintaining high quality products, and thereby developing one of the most loyal and productive work forces in existence.

"One time a huge batch of macaroni was slightly overcooked," says Woods. "They could have gone ahead and used it, but management decided not to and they called the entire work force together around the 'kettle'. They made a little speech about the importance of product quality and then dumped the whole batch down the drain."

It is this kind of demonstrated willingness to take a significant cost increase in order to maintain quality that drives belief in the concept home to employees.

Sharing company direction with workers? Yes. This type of management by consensus from all levels facilitates creativity and innovation. Management's role is as facilitator. Their job is to give employees the tools to improve quality and help channel worker efforts toward the ultimate corporate goal of higher profitability, which should naturally flow from meeting and surpassing customer expectations. ●••

10

Quality And The Employee Survey

What are employees' perceptions about the strengths and weaknesses of their company? Do they feel they have an open forum to express their views? What about working conditions, advancement opportunities, and compensation and benefits?

Just as the quality process often begins with a survey of external customers, it is helpful to take a reading of what the people working for an organization feel. There may be surprises for management if an opportunity is provided for people to set out constructive criticism or make suggestions without fear of reprisal. Too often, despite the appearance of openness, employees will hesitate to be candid in their assessment of what is going on. It may be safer to play the game and "tell them what they want to hear."

At Brauer Supply we distributed an employee opinion survey the day following our quality kick-off meeting. The following statement was addressed to all employees:

> "We are interested in your opinion about our company as a place to work. Your help is needed in making improvements. Please give your honest opinion on the following items. We are interested in group results only, thus you as an individual will remain anonymous. PLEASE DO NOT SIGN YOUR NAME. We will share the collective information with you in subsequent meetings."

We then followed with a series of thirty questions which gave people the chance to agree, disagree, or state that they had no opinion.

The questions were compiled from several similar surveys at other companies involved in the quality process and focused on such areas as advancement opportunities, company goals and missions, job security, ability to make a contribution, and distribution of workload. Following the specific statements, open-ended questions were asked to find out what things the employee would change at the company, how employee attitudes could be improved, and what the employees liked best about the company.

In short order we received responses back from almost all of the employees which corroborated most of our perceptions about employee attitudes. While results showed generally positive feelings there were expressions of discontent in some areas which caused us to focus on improvement where possible. In a few instances, people registered strong discontent, which may be inevitable when you have a large group, but which still directed our attention to areas which needed correction.

Employees are a great source of information to help get the quality process started.

"We were doing employee surveys long before people spoke about the term 'quality'," says IBM's Cay Bradley. Everyone at IBM takes the same basic survey but there are ten specific questions for departments. In the southern region they were asked specifically about quality and quality perceptions.

In a company dealing with changing markets such as IBM, feedback from the employees is extremely important. Because of the critical nature of this information, says Bradley, management is partially evaluated by these survey responses.

Consultant Don Kardux sees the employee survey as playing a key role in the planning and development of a TQM program.

Kardux recommends that each employee be interviewed at the start of the process. The survey is done confidentially so that ideas can be judged strictly on their merits. The ideas of the maintenance person will have equal weight with those of the president. He utilizes a seventeen question format composed of closed and open-ended questions. The final question is described as a "Pandora's Box" question (so named because you open a topic and anything can come out) which asks, "If you were an all-powerful genie and could make anything happen at our company with a wave of your hand, what three things would you cause to happen?"

It is surprising how many good ideas and suggestions are raised in response to this final question.

In designing a survey, Kardux asks questions to draw out information from employees in all company areas including:

1. *Administrative- dealing with all support functions.*
2. *Accounting- encompassing everything that is counted.*
3. *Marketing- whatever we do to get leads.*
4. *Sales- the process used to move a lead to actual work for the company.*
5. *Production- whatever the company does to earn money.*
6. *Physical Plant- the physical presence in the market area including bricks and mortar and everything inside, including the layout of work areas.*
7. *Management- anything we do to help the preceding six areas work best.*

Merely gathering information is meaningless unless the company takes steps to use the information and implement the ideas. This is management's responsibility along with the quality steering committee.

As part of his approach, Kardux helps companies create advisory boards composed of three separate groups: (1) Employees, (2) Vendors, and (3) People who know nothing about the business. The board schedules five meetings of exactly two hours duration during which they go through a process of internal analysis, market analysis, and goal setting for the company.

The internal analysis utilizes the results of the employee survey and places the various comments and conclusions on cards which are affixed to an easel board. The group decides if the interview statements merit action. The market analysis is straightforward, again using a card system. Management advises the board in what markets they are willing to do business and the board helps identify the company's niche. All competitors are identified and their gross dollar sales in the company's target niche are estimated and totaled to arrive at a temporary total market dollar figure.

Finally, the owners or management determines a gross dollar goal for the next year which flows from information developed from the market analysis and the analysis of current market share. With the goal established, the five or six critical things which must be done are agreed upon from the original idea board.

Total Quality stresses the role of the front-line workers in delivering services and meeting customer expectations. In effect, it sends the message that we are *all* front-line employees. The company's heart and soul is the people who do the work. Accordingly, no Total Quality process can succeed without a fair and true reading of their thoughts and opinions. Taking this true reading, and then organizing to use the results, can play a big role in determining whether those employees will feel a sense of ownership in the process or see it as a program imposed on them and far removed from reality. ●●•

11

Aligning The Organization To Support Quality

The implementation of a Total Quality Management process brings a new way of approaching daily tasks and solving problems. Sometimes new structures and procedures are put in place at the outset to insure that TQM will fit comfortably within the corporate framework.

Formalized structures to facilitate quality are most often evident in larger companies where the personal impact of a CEO's commitment to the process must be translated on down the line and reinforced through systems and procedures.

Let's take a look at a number of large companies which have ventured into the quality process in recent years and examine the changes which have come about to meet the program demands and see how they are adapting as the process continues to evolve. These companies are: Amana Refrigeration, Inc., McDonnell Douglas Corporation, the Principal Financial Group, and Southwestern Bell Telephone. All are acknowledged leaders in their fields and have achieved a reputation for quality products, yet they all have recognized a need to take a step beyond their current levels of quality assurance and institute formalized programs which are changing the way employees relate to customers and to each other. In some instances, the basic organizational structures of the companies have undergone revision.

● ISO 9000 at Amana

In early 1992, Amana Refrigeration, Inc. began implementing the ISO 9000 quality standard at its Fayetteville, Tennessee plant. The efforts of the entire facility were directed toward this goal and, by the end of the year, the company became the first in its industry in the United States to achieve registration by the American Gas Association Laboratories to the designated standard. With a reputation growing out of a century long history, the company focused its initial efforts on its heating and air conditioning products. The effort is now being expanded to its refrigeration, microwave, and other appliance products manufactured in Amana, Iowa. These are the products upon which the company, now a division of Raytheon, initially built its reputation.

"We have a separate Quality Department that functions in all areas of the factory," says quality assurance manager Bob Beck of the Fayetteville plant. "Each production department is, however, responsible for the quality of the product they produce."

Beck describes Amana's quality program as being structured on the ISO 9000 standard. Since this covers every area of the facility it provides a disciplined plan for running the entire business with a strong emphasis on continuous improvement. He says there were few changes at the outset of the program but there were many changes in how things were managed. The whole process involves a greater degree of documentation and employee involvement.

Top management's input is continually brought into the quality process through the review of internal audits, weekly quality meetings, and monthly operations review meetings, as well as periodic reports and briefings. A corrective action system, set forth in a quality manual, provides for effective and prompt correction of quality problems.

Responsibility for preventing errors and prompt correction is fixed on each employee and department through the procedures in the manual and directives in training meetings and employee reviews. This is reinforced by ongoing product audits which are conducted all day, every day, by a separate quality assurance group and engineering lab. Additionally, internal quality audits confirm the continuing effectiveness of the entire quality system.

"We have just begun to tap the potential of the ISO 9000 program," says Beck. "It has been a tremendous success story that has improved the quality of life as well as the quality of the products. We intend to build on that success."

● Quality at McDonnell Douglas

At McDonnell Douglas, the giant St. Louis and California based company which built its reputation on aerospace and defense, varied structures help to drive the quality program. This diversity is increasingly important as the company continues to expand its activities into new areas.

Staff Vice President for Quality Systems Ken Best describes the quality process as being managed by teams, the members of which are those individuals responsible for the application of given processes. Each of McDonnell's operations has a Quality Processes Organization, whose purpose is to accelerate the implementation of TQM in the businesses it serves. The team concept is prevalent throughout McDonnell and provides much of the structure of their quality efforts. The nature of McDonnell's industry literally requires that there be a quality department in their organizational structure. Government, customer contracts, and specifications drive that requirement.

"Structurally, the quality assurance function may or may not be a department within the Quality Processes Division," says Best. "That decision is driven by what makes the most sense for our customers, taking into account their expectations. Regardless, our approach to TQM makes quality every department's responsibility."

Best says McDonnell's approach to TQM was specifically developed by the company's executive management as part of their vision, defined mission, and corporate values. One of the strategic business objectives designated by top management is quality. Accordingly, they have used the Malcolm Baldrige National Quality Award criteria as a template for planning and evaluating their journey toward Total Quality Management.

McDonnell has established problem-solving processes for both the white collar and production areas. These processes are very disciplined in character and begin by identifying the root cause of the problem, identifying solutions, and verifying the effectiveness of action taken.

"We have reduced the complexity and number of our policies and procedures to help streamline our work," said Best. " A flattening of our organization has empowered more people and reduced the red tape that accompanies multiple layers of management."

Best described how each operating division of the company has an integrated business plan which includes both a strategic and tactical quality plan. These plans are "rolled down" in those operations with specific goals and performance measures that can be identified at the department level. Individual performance objectives are also derived from that process which include specific quality improvement objectives with performance measures as well. The TQM assessment process provides performance objectives for virtually all employees that link to the company's quality plans and strategic business objectives.

What impact did the adoption of a quality program have on McDonnell's organizational structure at the outset?

Best says that every operating division reorganized at the beginning and there have been several changes since then. To a certain extent this would have occurred anyway because of the shrinkage of the defense industry. Many of these necessary changes overlapped changes driven by the push for Total Quality Management. Nevertheless, TQM has proven to be a prime consideration in how new structures are created and the quality change agents have continued to be an integral element of the new structures.

McDonnell Douglas is typical of many large companies in that it is characterized by multiple operating divisions, and in fact, by many companies operating under a larger corporate umbrella. This raises many questions about the applicability of the quality process to companies with various business objectives.

"Our companies share the same principles," says Best. "Our model for TQM requires us to be focused on the customer."

Best says the use of disciplined processes and systems, team concepts, and a supportive cultural environment are constant throughout the McDonnell companies. Also, the use of the Baldrige criteria guides thinking about the approach to TQM and it is within those parameters that the operating units pursue total quality.

Of particular importance in the McDonnell program is the development of an "Enterprise Process" model that applies to the defense companies. The use of that model should naturally provide for more integration of approaches to TQM in the future. Finally, McDonnell has a Process Improvement Council that is empowered to drive process improvements in a common fashion across the operations. That council uses a structured approach to process improvement that has become the standard throughout McDonnell.

"For effective integration of quality throughout an organization structure, top management committment, if not obsession, is required," says Best. "Nothing is as precarious as change. TQM by its nature is characterized by continuous change. It is senior management's job to insure alignment and stay the course."

● The Principal Focuses on Customers

The Principal Financial Group, located in Des Moines, is a leading national provider of employee benefit , life insurance, and financial products for individuals and corporations. The nature of their ultimate customer causes them to equate "quality" to a focus on customer needs, wants, and expectations.

The company is organized into a number of business units and markets within those units, done so that they would be responsive to the particular needs of the marketplace.

"We have carried this philosophy into our internal customer/supplier chain as well, although it does not always work as well internally due to economies of scale," says Duane Brinkman who is director of management services. "Many of our people are organized into teams and serve a given block of customers and, in some cases, an individual is responsible for a given group of customers which brings the issue of service quality and knowing customer expectations to the desk of the person who delivers the service."

Rather than a company-wide quality department, each area at The Principal is responsible for the quality of the work they produce. They typically do not call their efforts "programs," but try to treat all improvement efforts as a part of the culture.

Brinkman's Management Services Department is available to consult with people in areas choosing to pursue quality and service initiatives.

The structure at The Principal is based on a combination of customer focus and the products offered. For example, a single customer may have individual life policies, mutual funds, and coverage for medical insurance, as well as a pension through The Principal. Because each area is responsible for its own quality and business results, there has been little corporate-wide restructuring resulting from the quality issue.

Given the financial nature of this business, the corporate auditing function pays attention to the consistency of process and controls and from this perspective, gets to the issue of quality. Various areas of the company have more sophisticated, statistically correct methods of sampling work or stand-alone units that review procedural quality, as well as the quality level that customers would be experiencing.

Noting that the company has many business units, each of which is extensively empowered, the things they do to insure quality vary based on that unit's situation, says Brinkman.

"We use a number of formal, as well as informal, networks to share ideas. Our cutomer service network, for example, has representatives from all business units and meets monthly to compare notes and talk about 'Best Practices'," says Brinkman. "We are also in the process of producing a data base of 'Best Practices' within The Principal to facilitate the deployment of ideas."

Brinkman predicts that his company will continue to do things to make it easier for customers to feel like they are doing business with one entity. With the large quantity of products offered he sees this as an ongoing challenge which may call for structural solutions.

● "Excellence Through Quality" at Southwestern Bell

At Southwestern Bell Corporation, the regional provider of telecommunication services, the decision as to whether or not to have a structured quality program is left up to the various subsidiary companies. Each organizational entity is responsible for its own implementation, with the pace and flavor of the programs varied as each company sees fit.

The largest subsidiary, Southwestern Bell Telephone, has adopted a program themed "Excellence Through Quality."

"Each market area has their own quality resource personnel," says Area Quality Manager Mike Berry. "These people report into the line management. Everything is aligned so quality can be an integral part of all activities."

A small centralized quality department, staffed by five full time managers, works on developing training, planning, and coordinating activities throughout the company. This department tracks improvement and maintains statistical data regarding quality improvement.

One hallmark of the "Excellence Through Quality" program is that the focus has been on moving the decision-making process closer to customers.

"Our strategy is to start with the processes in the company which are closest to the customer and work backwards from these to get the most bang for our quality buck," says Berry. "Accordingly," he said, "quality resource personnel are sprinkled throughout the line organization."

Two levels of quality personnel are involved, those who have been intensively schooled in quality processes and those trained to a lesser degree.

"Niney per cent of our quality resources are spread throughout the organization," says Berry.

● Conclusion

One of the problems often cited with the implementation of Total Quality is the tendency to create unnecessary committees, structures, and paperwork, and that too much time is spent in meetings. A clear cut and well-defined structure should help to keep these problems to a minimum. The entities responsible for making the quality program go—the steering committee, action teams, those responsible for monitoring and charting quality activity, become in some sense an organization within an organization. It is important that this new structure's activities be consistent and coordinated with that of the company as a whole. The quality functionaries should serve as a catalyst for the entire organization to achieve higher levels of performance and should complement rather than conflict with the goals of senior management.

A small business, while lacking the resources of a larger enterprise, will have the advantage of a management that is "closer to the action" and the CEO will have the opportunity to put his personal imprint on the company's culture. In the large company, however, structure and systems become critical.

The methods of facilitating a successful quality process vary from company to company—yet—a common thread runs through all programs. Efforts are made to bring all decisions closer to the customer, to ensure that the end product (be it services or goods) is a mirror of the customer's expectations.

To the extent that the structure of an organization impedes that goal, it must be modified. To the extent that it helps achieve that end, it must be reinforced.

Perceiving which is which and then acting upon it is the first duty of management. ●●•

12

Selling The
Quality Concept
To Employees

The need for Total Quality in all phases of a company's operations may be readily apparent to top management. It may have been drilled into the team chosen to attend a quality improvement seminar. It may even be a concept welcomed by the sales force looking for an edge in marketing products to the customer base.

For the most part, however, the average employee has been going along quite comfortably with things the way they are and has to be shown some reason to change his or her way of looking at the job. It is therefore incumbent on those developing the program to consider just how the program will be communicated to the employees who will be asked to carry it out.

What is involved here is a basic change in corporate culture. This is not a simple endeavor. Timing as well as method is important. Approaching the employees at a time when they are fatigued, demoralized, or burned out can result in failure of a quality campaign.

It will be crucial to have the support and readiness of all people in the organization. This means that the program must appeal to people on an emotional as well as an intellectual level.

The quality steering committee bears the responsibility to develop a plan to communicate the quality policy which will tell employees what will be done, when it will happen, and what will be expected of them. The introduction should make it clear that the business will be run henceforth in a "quality" manner and that each employee is expected to sign up in the effort.

Many companies find that a carefully orchestrated "kick-off" event is effective. Curiosity and interest can be piqued by "teaser" announcements, posters, notes with paychecks, and letters to employees' homes. The kick-off meeting should be run in a first class manner setting the tone for the entire program. Many companies find it helpful to hold it off premises with a dinner or refreshments provided along with motivational speeches, explanations of the program, introduction of the steering committee, and explanation of the quality policy.

The effectiveness of the kick-off and communication campaign can be measured by the degree of enthusiasm and excitement prevailing in an organization's employees. As the program unfolds, more quantifiable measurements will be needed, but it is indeed true that the program must start off with commitment of the hearts of an organization's workers.

To this end, it is imperative that top management be highly visible and play a key role in the beginning events. Since some may view the program as "corny" and be inclined to question its worth, the imprint of senior management helps to insure that middle managers and supervisors give their full commitment to the concept.

Communicating the program to employees takes many different forms.

At Honeywell, the employee rally came after the program was put into effect. An outdoor gathering with barbecue and a band celebrated the successful launching of the program which had been developed by an executive team as an antidote to difficulties which had been plaguing the company, says Jim Widtfeldt, manager of quality integration for the Home and Building Systems Controls Division.

"Our quality programs started in 1982," says Widtfeldt. "We've been at it for ten years and celebrate Quality Appreciation Day every October. This is a time for rededication to our quality commitment."

At IBM, quality has been a focus since the early 1980's, says Cay Bradley.

Since 1988 IBM has worked to implement "Market Driven Quality" (MDQ). This approach has been used company-wide to help employees recognize that it is the market, the customers, who define whether the quality of products and services are satisfactory, superior, or not acceptable. The market driven quality plan was announced in a video distributed to every IBM office world-wide.

According to Bradley, IBM has established ongoing quality programs which vary by business focus area. Bradley herself represents a business unit of eight people. In the Wholesale Distribution Industry group, IBM'ers participate on process teams to improve specific business functions, such as information delivery.

Bradley cited special classes she taught to introduce company employees throughout the southeastern states to quality. The classes were designed to help them deal with change and take on responsibility. Techniques for improving teamwork and emphasizing customer satisfaction and product quality are taught.

Further down the chain, IBM has instituted programs for their vendors and re-sellers which emphasize Total Quality in the entire product delivery system. Vendors are encouraged to participate in the "Mark of Quality" team programs.

Dave Whiting, president of General Data Systems, Inc. (with four midwestern locations), has brought his organization under the umbrella of this program and has actively worked to involve his employees. People from his various departments meet regularly with the steering committee as part of monthly informal gatherings. He participates in all of these meetings which are characterized as "pizza with Dave." These meetings have encouraged give and take from employees at all levels on problem resolution and have helped to bring all workers into the quality process.

IBM provides an evaluation and rating to their participating vendors, like General Data, to assist in building quality programs based on the Malcolm Baldrige Quality Award guidelines. The IBM facility in Rochester, Minnesota, previously won the Baldrige Award and, following that, developed this program as part of the ongoing responsibility which rests upon award winners.

Pitfalls which management may face in communicating a quality policy include the problem of short attention spans, where managers and employees become distracted by the more immediate day-to-day problems. Top management itself may be initially excited about the concept after attendance at a training seminar but may be failing to follow through. Management credibility suffers when employees begin to view this as just one more fad which will fade away.

Slogans, mottos, and catch phrases which do not relate to actual steps for quality improvement will tend to destroy credibility of a program. Likewise, overly rigid control systems and excessive reports and paperwork can tie up the creative forces which a company is seeking to unleash and kill enthusiasm quickly.

"It's important for management to realize that people will be skeptical because they've seen programs come and go," says Honeywell's Widtfeldt. "They need to be shown what makes this different from all other events and programs."

Management must demonstrate support for the quality concept over time. Executives not willing to make this long-term commitment should be doing something else, for the organization's workers will follow their lead and quality efforts will be doomed to failure. ●●•

Reports From The Front Lines.

Aspects of
Quality

13

Quality And Change

"Young man, let me show you something that's going to change the way people do business!"

It was 1973 and it was my first day of work at a large midwestern bank. Just out of law school, I was starting an orientation program, spending time in all the major departments. The gentleman who was about to let me in on this "secret" was a veteran of the accounting department.

He opened his desk drawer and took out a small leather case from which he produced a little black gadget with number pads on it and a small window display. He pushed a plastic switch on the side and little red numerals danced across the top of the device. Almost with reverence he began to calculate addition, subtraction, and multiplication problems.

"In a few years every manager will have one of these on his desk," he predicted.

It was the first digital hand-held calculator I had seen and, to be honest (not being particularly enamored with numbers at the time), I don't believe I fully grasped the significance of what had just been demonstrated. This fellow who had spent his career working with mechanical adding machines on his desk sensed that big changes were about to happen and he was excited about the prospect!

I often think back to that day and ponder how important it is to "catch the wave" when change is afoot. How many of our companies have stumbled because they missed the boat when faced with new technology or changing markets?

The company involved in the Total Quality process should have an edge in preparing for change. The openness and free exchange of information promoted by the process should help the company avoid getting into the trap of "We've always done it this way" and should provide a fertile field for trying any reasonable new process, procedure, or equipment.

"The involvement of everyone in the quality process leads to freedom of ideas," says Steve Wikstrom of Reell Precision Manufacturing in St. Paul. "You'll have the collective horsepower of a hundred people rather than just a select few."

Tom Tener, vice president of Maritz Motivation Company agrees that the existence of TQM in a company opens up all kinds of opportunities for dealing with new ideas and concepts. This is particularly true in meeting the changing needs of customers.

"From our perspective, what we did yesterday for our clients isn't good enough," says Tener. "What we did yesterday becomes the standard. As an incentive company it means the next trip or merchandise will be judged against that which we provided last year. Our ability to deliver to the clients must exceed their expectations today and also what we did yesterday."

Tener is responsible for the ongoing employee involvement program at Maritz. The aim of the program is to put money on the bottom line by tapping into employee ideas. Coming from a background in the training and human resource area, Tener was selected after a strategic decision to separate the quality process from all other departments. The idea was that the process should not be the exclusive product of any established department.

Tener points to an example of change within his organization— the total re-engineering of jobs undertaken at the company. This would not have been possible, he says, without a quality process. Going in and making no assumptions about anything, starting from ground zero, flows directly from total quality principles.

When it comes to change, people often confuse cause and effect in quality management.

"We may say we need to get more people involved, so a program is put together, thinking it will be a cause for improvement," says Southwestern Bell Telephone's Mike Berry. "If we do things right, however, employee involvment will be a result and not a cause of quality improvement."

Customer needs are also a constantly changing item, or as some say, the customer is a moving target. How do you keep your aim on this target?

"We talk to our customers and do a lot of surveying but don't always ask the right question," says Berry. "We try to put the emphasis on observing customers and not just talking to them."

Berry cited examples such as the Honda Company, which took new cars to the Disney World parking lot and invited people to inspect the vehicles. Honda managers just watched and asked no questions. Watching customers interact with the product or service sometimes can reveal more about customer expectations than can interviewing because the observer is more likely to pick up on small details of reactions and he or she is not focused on formulating the next question.

Tener also cautions against "surveying the customer to death."

"We view the relationship with our clients as a partnership . . . we want to be long-term strategic partners to fulfill their goals and to motivate their customers and to help them meet the changing needs of their markets. In this way we stay close to our clients and are aware of the changes they face."

Are attitudes about customer service changing as a result of the Total Quality movement?

Tener says emphatically yes! There has been so much written, he says, that people expect world-class service and products.

"The world has changed so much that people expect good service and that products will work," says Tener. "When these things don't happen they are offended."

Wikstrom says his company has seen a marked change in their suppliers. They are starting to make quality demands on their own vendors and are focusing on the expectation of excellent service. He remembers that in years past his company was somewhat of an evangelist for Total Quality and stood alone as a practitioner of the process.

"The gap is closing from where we are and where our suppliers are," says Wikstrom. "People see quality and the resulting customer service as fundamentally crucial to their success."

At Southwestern Bell, Berry says the company and its predecessors have always had a strong focus on customer service. With TQM, however, they are looking more at customer needs rather than the company's own definition of customer service. Everything is being redefined from the customer's own definition.

In the measured process of Total Quality, readiness and response to change has overtones of scientific analysis, but is there room for acting on instinct and gut feelings about changing needs of the marketplace?

"My experience would say that sometimes change calls upon us to be open to ideas that may be correct, but cannot be substantiated by hard data," says Berry. "Don't shout them down. Help them analyze why they believe a particular idea will work and see if a trial run will yield the necessary evidence to support or reject the idea."

If a shift in position is necessary and there is no data to back it up, that data must be established somewhere and therefore the idea can be instituted on a limited basis to begin to create evidence as to its viability.

"Creative ideas need to be discussed and tested," says Precisionaire's Bill Beck.

Maritz's Tener comes down on the side of data and market information. Without sufficient data there is a risk that changes may result in excessive cost or may not meet customer's real needs.

Berry agrees that decisions should be based on data but the "gut instinct" response to change comes in deciding the issues on which to work.

"Instinct points us in the right direction," he says. "Back up data and evidence is developed to see if that direction is taking us where we want to go. It is important that a company not hesitate to change direction if situations change or results are not being obtained."

Identifying and learning the new process that will provide a competitive edge makes everyone a strategist.

Change can be threatening or it can be an opportunity. The quality oriented company will see that its people are constantly reviewing industry literature and periodicals, attending trade shows and listening to the presentations of salespeople to prepare for the new ideas and opportunities that constantly surround companies today.

Exponential change is a fact we must deal with if our companies are to survive in today's marketplace. Viewing it as a chance to find better methods, however, means it is not something to be feared, but a welcome opportunity. The quality process itself is an example of that change.

Will you and your business be ready? ●●•

14

Partnering In
The Quality Process

A chain is only as strong as its weakest link . . . and the organization that neglects a link in its chain of product or service delivery will surely fail to achieve its maximum level of quality.

Therefore, the company setting out on the road to Total Quality must view those who play a part in putting together the final product as partners rather than adversaries. This includes vendors of raw materials and services as well as external professionals such as lawyers, accountants, insurers, and bankers. While the focus of a quality process remains on the internal structure of a company and the development of a "quality culture," these external partners have a key role to play.

Vendors, in particular, are an important but sometimes difficult component.

"Part of the problem is that vendors have a great deal of impact on a company's final product, but prior to the implementation of a quality program there has never been a formal process to get their input," says David Gleason, New York based consultant and president of Systematic Selling, Inc.

Gleason, a former contractor, wholesaler, trade association president, and training director for a national chain of hardware distributors, provides a structured quality program built upon a sixteen week process aimed at changing a company culture from its present state into what will become its culture of the future.

Gleason says this process involves inviting partners such as raw material manufacturers and service providers to a quality workshop where they become active participants in a company's program.

"These people bring good ideas and suggestions to the quality steering committee," he says. "It's amazing how people who are associates of an organization really begin to feel they are part of the company when they have a chance to really have input."

Gleason reports that levels of participation by outside vendors vary, generally dependent upon the outsider's awareness of the quality process.

"Some sixty per cent to seventy per cent of those outside professionals accepting invitations to attend workshops have quality programs within their own organizations. Rather than being cynical, they welcome this strengthening of bonds with their customer or client."

The best results are obtained when two organizations with a focus on quality are welded together. They are compatible because they are thinking on the same wave length and using the same language. Interaction between the partners is increased.

Part of the whole quality process, of course, focuses on resolving weaknesses in a company and suggestions for change may involve a vendor. Having the supplier as a partner in the process makes it easier for people in the organization to work with the outside company to resolve the situation.

Vendor quality ratings and compliance with procedures often are enhanced when the vendor is actively brought into the culture.

Some managers instituting quality are concerned that the supplier will use the existence of the quality program and the demands it places on them as justification for charging a higher price. Gleason asserts that this will not happen if true communication is open between the parties. When the purchasing company asks for a price to be competitive in a market the supplier will have a better understanding of the need and, likewise, the buyer will recognize the need for the manufacturer/supplier to operate making a profit.

Strategic "win-win" relationships can be fostered by setting up consulting councils of suppliers or customers to advise a company on effective products or service development.

Jerry Shafer, vice president of sales for Consolidated Industries Corporation in Lafayette, Indiana, has recently been involved in setting up a series of "distributor advisory councils" and "contractor focus groups" for the multi-brand manufacturer of furnaces. This utilizing of participants in the chain of distribution to the ultimate consumer as sounding boards is a growing phenomenon in the spreading quality culture.

"We're trying to find out what are our customers' needs," says Shafer. "Our mission statement established that we are a customer driven company and, by partnering with distributors and contractors, we are better able to identify the conditions of the market and the competitive environment."

Shafer says the councils are a resource to clarify what constitutes the market and to define objectives. Once this is determined he sees his company's job as designing and implementing programs to reach those objectives.

Consolidated's suppliers play a role in this process also. Shafer points to Honeywell, who supplies controls to Consolidated, and who provides training resources and literature.

"We are approaching all of our vendors to support our drive for quality and success in the market," says Shafer.

Indeed, for many companies the road to quality is through ensuring quality of their supplier's products and delivery. Standards are developed to which suppliers are held and ratings set up which, if not attained, result in dropping the given vendor. One problem this may lead to is a rigid and inflexible termination of what could be a productive relationship if the requirements are not well thought out or correctly communicated to the vendor.

In fact, the three most frequent reasons for the failure of a supplier partnership, as noted by Kevin Beidelman, Director of Supplier Quality and Procurement for Newport/Klinger of Irvine, California, are:

1. *The failure of purchasing to get management's blessing at the outset of a partnership.*

2. *Insufficient planning by purchasing as to how it wants to proceed with its partnering program.*

3. *When suppliers themselves are questioning whether they will receive any benefit from the relationship.*[1]

Some companies are compelled by circumstances to deal in partnership with a labor union. While this presents some unique problems it is still possible to build a foundation for co-operation in the pursuit of quality.

When a company is unionized the quality process will probably take longer to become part of the culture. The union will want to know what's in it for them. The answer is that the success of the process will bring better communication between management and union.

Just as commitment to the quality process must be on a long term basis, so must the parties view the partnering relationship as an alliance designed for the long haul. This differs from a long-term contract which still sets the parties in an adversarial relationship guided by mutual obligations. The partnering relationship, while still ideally based on a written understanding, is focused more on the development of trust and support rather than mutual obligation. It is centered on cooperation rather than competition. It is characterized by openness, free exchange of ideas, and a commitment to sharing information.

Clearly, in an era of limited resources and broader geographical markets, companies can compete successfully only by using all resources they can bring to bear. Building strategic partnerships with organizations with whom they regularly deal can help marshal those resources to reach objectives.

The integration of strategic partnering into the quality process brings all players into the effort to successfully meet customer requirements. ●●●

15

*Keeping
The Customer
In Mind*

"**I**f the customers don't like the way I dress, maybe we should get new customers!"

I stared incredulously at the warehouse employee whom I was attempting to counsel about the need to present a business-like appearance. We seemed to be speaking different languages. To his way of thinking, if he carried out the specific functions of his job, he was doing what he was hired to do and if his work brought him into contact with a customer it was really irrelevant what kind of impression he made. He just saw no connection between pleasing customers and his own job security. It was up to the customers to accept him as he was.

Too often we have failed to address the importance of every employee at every level of an organization having an understanding of the need to attract and hold customers if a company is to survive and prosper. Whether dealing with engineers, researchers, executives or janitors, the company's and the individual's mission must somehow be related to the customer who is the reason for the job's existence.

Studies have shown that fewer than four per cent of customers who have had a bad experience at a company will report it and over ninety per cent of those who do make their complaints known will not come back. Worse, the person who has been "burned" will likely tell some ten to twenty people about the experience. For the company whose people confront the problem head-on, there is some hope, however. The same research reports that, depending on the industry, some eighty-two to ninety-five per cent of the customers can be won back by resolving their complaints in a timely fashion.[1]

How critical it is, then, to encourage all employees to develop customer awareness and a sense of urgency in providing top-flight service!

"Stressing customer consciousness goes way back to the days before we began institutionalizing it in the quality movement," says Honeywell's Jim Widtfeldt. "It just has to be a natural part of the corporate culture."

This concern for the customer must start at the top if people up and down the line are expected to give their full commitment. If management exists in an ivory tower and does not concern itself with how people on the front line are relating to the customer then you can expect a "who cares" attitude to creep into the organization.

It has often been said that a customer complaint is an opportunity. That may be a cliche, but it certainly does present a chance to demonstrate management's commitment to customers by promptly and visibly attending to the problem in such a manner that an example is set for all other employees.

Suppose, for example, that a CEO is about to gather a meeting of department heads to work out details of a new procedure. Fifteen minutes before the meeting he becomes aware of a botched order and a valued customer whose production line is shut down because of it. If the boss delegates someone to attend to the problem rather than giving it his immediate attention he is sending a message not only to the distressed customer but to his own management team also. What a powerful example if, instead of proceeding with the planned meeting, he puts things on hold and rushes to contact the customer and involve himself in insuring a quick resolution to the situation!

Management commitment and symbolic action are important, but what about specific training in customer responsiveness? How should it be structured and who should do the teaching? Is it enough just to create the proper workplace atmosphere?

At Maritz, Inc., the St. Louis based employee incentive and motivation company which specializes in personnel productivity, training in customer responsiveness varies depending on whether the targeted employees serve internal (within the company itself) or external customers.

Maritz's Director of Employee Training and Development Karin Barker says they use the concept of "Leading Excellent Service" developed from the writings of Len Barry, in training the company's own managers.

"We take the managers through a wheel, the various spokes of which are different components of customer service," says Barker.

Maritz uses the following process to help employees achieve service excellence:

1. *Assess who the customers are.*

2. *Assess the customer needs.*

3. *Put management systems into place to meet those needs.*

4. *Determine how managers lead those efforts.*

5. *Determine what kind of reinforcements can be put into place to insure continuance.*

Hiring for excellence as well as training is important, says Barker.

Most of all, they try to give employees the skills and the decision-making latitude to meet customer needs on the spot.

"Our systems and behaviors must be aligned with the customer's requirements," says Widtfeldt. "We need to break down the focus on function where a manager or a department is thinking that they've got a specific piece of the action and don't see it as part of the delivery of services to the ultimate customer."

Widtfeldt cited the use of specific devices such as 800 numbers, special account representatives, and customer service seminars as visible symbols reinforcing concern for the consumer. He said the quality training programs developed at Honeywell include immediate contacts by telephone with real customers, either external or internal, to find out what the requirements actually are and how they can be met.

Curiously, when I contacted another major national company concerning their training in customer satisfaction the training department officials kept transferring me higher up the corporate ladder for comments. I finally was referred to their advertising agency for a statement. One would think this concept would be on the tip of every trainer's tongue!

Employees need immediate feedback on errors or actions which impact negatively on customers. Reports of mistaken shipments, less than polite service or failure to return phone calls promptly should be immediately discussed with the employee and plans made for corrective action. If supervisors shrug off a certain number of errors as unavoidable or within a tolerable percentage they are sending a message that meeting customer requirements is not the highest priority. If a passionate desire for perfection is communicated to employees along with the knowledge that they will have to be involved in cleaning up problems resulting from their mistakes then employees will be concerned with preventing problems before they occur.

Employees joining our companies today may well be the product of an educational system, media influence, and a culture which has not instilled a respect for authority. It may fall to us to teach them respect for that ultimate authority—the customer—if they want to be able to enjoy some of the good things life has to offer! ●●·

16

Recognition And Reward In The Quality Process

Successful sales people are usually driven by a strong ego and an urge to gain recognition for their accomplishments. It is just that trait that has generally led them to work in the sales field and the savvy manager designs compensation and recognition programs to meet that need.

When an organization begins to develop a quality improvement process it is dealing with its entire employee base. Some of those employees have very different personalities from members of the sales force and may have an entirely different set of "hot" buttons. Nevertheless, a system of reward for compliance with the process and for suggestions to raise quality levels should be an integral part of any company's quality agenda.

Rewards to employees come on two levels—enhanced self-esteem as they become more productive at their work and, alternatively, specific tangible rewards to foster achievement of short term goals and to put a little zip into the program.

Should reward systems be separate and apart from the company's compensation program or should they be rolled into the overall package?

While subjective evaluation of an individual's participation and involvement in quality efforts should be taken into consideration in setting salary levels, many companies find it effective to set up short term "spiffs" or prizes to provide a structure to the process. There are some who would call these "bribes" to get employees to do what they should do of their own volition, but if the value of the rewards is small they can serve to merely add a bit of excitement to the process and let employees know that this is a different sort of endeavor.

"We think incentives have their place in QIP," says Tom Tener, who is vice president of Maritz Continuous Improvement Systems. "We are convinced that people are motivated to improve in both large and small ways by having rewards available."

Probably the most critical thing is to ensure that the right accomplishments are being rewarded. When recognition and compensation are disbursed for meaningless peripheral efforts it merely serves to focus employees on those nonproductive actions or to make a mockery of the quality program. Recognition and rewards must be for meaningful accomplishments and they must have value both materially and psychologically to the person receiving them.

Should the rewards be part of a systematic program? Yes. If specific criteria are set forth to establish how awards are to be earned then everyone will have an opportunity to pursue the incentive. This does not mean that spur-of-the-minute awards cannot be given for good ideas, helpful suggestions, or outstanding effort if such presentation (with appropriate fanfare) can encourage comparable creative effort by others, but the system should be in place to recognize the dogged persistence of the employee slugging away at repetitive tasks.

In implementing a quality program at our distribution company in St. Louis, we set forth three 30 day programs for specific improvement in meeting the expectations of specifically identified internal customers. Each employee was involved in exercises to achieve measurable results in the eyes of that customer. Small rewards such as baseball tickets, dinner certificates, and grocery coupons were offered to those who met the 30 day improvement criteria. Participation goals were set for the entire company for the end of the 90 days and, when met, the entire organization was rewarded with a day at a local theme park. The rewards represented a small percentage of individuals' compensation, but it did give the program a focus and a "gamesmanship" aspect that brought more active participation.

Beyond specific tangible rewards, systems can be set up for peer recognition and recognition from managers and the quality steering committee. These can be such things as engraving names on plaques for display in public areas, posting of employee photos, special parking spots, or recognition in company-wide memos or newsletters.

"The size and scope of the rewards should be reflective of the size and scope of the impact of the employee's efforts," says Tener. "If it is improvement in a small area then perhaps a lunch with the boss (if it fits into the culture) is effective, but large improvements with tangible impact on the bottom line merit significant tangible rewards."

Tener stressed that quality efforts and bottom line results cannot be separated.

Setting the reward system can be a function of the quality steering committee or a special sub-committee which should include managers and line workers. The involvement of employees in creating recommendations for rewards can ensure they are things which will appeal to the group. This group can also serve as an evaluation committee for suggestions and ideas which have been submitted.

In line with the overall quality guidelines, the recognition should be made in a timely fashion after the activity has occurred.

If rewards are instituted properly they will give that extra sizzle to the quality campaign and make the whole process an enjoyable experience for employees. As long as the goal remains fixed on the substance of QIP and the main reward comes from the personal satisfaction employees will feel, then the reward system will be kept in its proper perspective.

If rewards are judiciously used, then goals will be achieved more rapidly, there will be an increase in employee suggestions which lead to quality improvement, and morale and job satisfaction will increase.

The ultimate test is, of course, how are the customers reacting? Are they reporting a noticeable difference when they interact with your employees?

To be more than sloganeering, the quality effort must continue over a long period of time so that it cannot be focused too much on gimmicks and incentives. For generating excitement about the campaign's kickoff, however, and getting the attention of less than enthusiastic workers, a simple system of rewards can make a big difference! ●●•

17

Quality By The Numbers?

When one surveys the available literature and checks out the various quality training programs advertised it becomes very apparent that quality as a process is viewed from two completely different perspectives. One group sees the whole endeavor as part of a teamwork and human relations program in which some kind of state of group self-actualization takes place whereby people realize their true potential for creative production and perfect quality work. The other group would reduce everything to statistics and numbers in a relentless pursuit of perfection.

The first can get a little vague in its aims and invites cynical responses from the more practical accountants, scientists, and engineers whose participation will be critical to the success of the process. On the other hand, relying solely on numbers ignores the fact that products and services are delivered by people—and leadership and willing commitment are required to produce those sought after results!

From conversations with people on both sides of this debate, I sometimes see a pattern where managers in large organizations tilt toward the statistical side and small business people talk in terms of "commitment" and personal service to customers. This may be a natural outgrowth of the staff resources available to the various types of organizations. Large companies might devote entire departments to statistical monitoring and the development of information to measure performance, whereas the small enterprise may be of such a size that the owner/manager can personally observe what is going on and have a true feel for the service levels actually being provided.

Where the two sometimes come into conflict is when the small business serves the larger as a vendor and must respond to the formal requirements of the large corporate customer. With some frequency quality control departments of large organizations send out forms and requests for information with instructions and questions conveyed in a jargon (complete with acronyms) that has doubtless become standard communication fare within that large company's culture but which needs an interpreter for vendors and those outside of the organization. In other words, assumptions are made that the internal quality culture existing at an enterprise is representative of the entire business world when such is not the case. Learning to interpret these requests for information and respond in the familiar jargon is a challenge, one that hopefully can lead to profits for these small businesses if successfully met.

Somewhere down the line a happy medium will be struck between these two views of TQM because, according to most architects of quality plans, there is room for and, in fact, need for emphasis on both.

"I don't believe you truly have a effective Total Quality process without both the statistical process control procedures and the human/teamwork aspect," says Scott Dickerhoff, senior product development engineer for the Anesthesiology Department of Mallinkrodt Medical, Inc. and a member of their quality improvement team. "However, if you have good human leadership and teamwork in place the other things will follow."

The application of a system of measurement to quality efforts is always regarded as a key component of the process, yet in non-manufacturing companies this can be difficult.

"Measuring in our wholesale distribution industry is extremely difficult," says President Jerry Peterson of Mortemp, Inc. in Seattle. "There are very few things you can measure finitely, though efforts are certainly made to track order-fill rates, back order percentages, and other ratios."

Peterson comes down strongly on the side of the primary importance of the leadership role in the development of a Total Quality process, stressing that if a company develops teamwork it will carry over into how a company meets its customers' expectations and will result in specific improvement.

At Mallinkrodt Medical, Inc., says Dickerhoff, individuals are trained in the Juran Quality Improvement Procedures. He notes that as a manufacturer of medical device type products their manufacturing process is highly regulated by the Food and Drug Administration and compliance to Good Manufacturing Practices (GMP) is required.

Outside consultants from the Juran Institute have been utilized to present different forms of training such as facilitator training, leader training, and training in the Juran Process for Team Members. This program stresses a balance between quantitative and leadership/human skills.

"In my opinion," says Dickerhoff, "you can't have a successful process without both aspects, however, you must have the leadership base established to effectively use and train people in these statistical/quantitative issues."

At Parker-Kalon, the manufacturer of threaded fasteners, Quality Assurance Supervisor Jo Ellen Lemmon says, "You can have all the numbers in the world and show them every process in the world, but if the human relationships aren't there the customers won't care!"

Lemmon does, however, believe each aspect of quality programs could stand alone, producing benefits for the company. Statistical process control by itself could improve some processes but its impact would be limited without combining it with TQM oriented toward the customer.

She explains that at the Campbellsville, Kentucky, plant of this subsidiary of Black and Decker, her role as coordinator of quality is integrated with department personnel who administer SPC and who have responsibility for interfacing these processes with TQM. Their quality program is totally developed in house at the Black and Decker companies and coordinated at each division under a general set of guidelines.

At Mortemp, Peterson is entering the fourth year of his program and has utilized periodic outside speakers of a motivational nature in addition to training from his own quality steering committee.

Measurement of specific improvements, and of return on the cost of quality, is important to the company evaluating whether or not its quality process is being carried out effectively. If only the leadership and team issues are stressed then no one would be qualified to implement an effective measurement system. Without training in statistical process control, results might not be interpreted correctly or the process might be set up wrong.

With written resources and outside advisors readily available it is logical that a company should use all of the tools available for success. A balance between the two approaches is vital.

Like Peterson, at Brauer Supply Company we have found the hardest part of a quality process is measurement. The sometimes intangible nature of the value-added services provided by a wholesale-distributor make it difficult to quantify results. Nevertheless, modern computer systems and diligent record-keeping can keep one clued in to key performance levels. What is often lacking is the self-discipline to stay with the measurement and utilize results as a basis for action.

In a small business it is too easy to form a subjective conclusion from conversations with employees and/or customers while ignoring actual results and trends demonstrated by the numbers. Perhaps part of the reason is that numbers sometimes present us with truths that we choose not to confront, preferring to cling to our own preconceived notions of what is really happening in our companies and in our marketplace.

The balance between statistics and human relations in the quality process is a delicate one and the process is ever changing. New factors are constantly being introduced which change both the statistical results and the need to reinterpret them or change the emphasis or style of leadership of the program.

"These programs cannot run on auto pilot," says Dickerhoff.

To be successful, the TQ process must be nurtured by constant human interaction supported and given direction by measurement of performance. The whole thing ties into the concept of goals discussed in an earlier chapter. Without statistical measurement you won't know where you are, won't know if you are moving in the right direction, and won't know where you want to go next after you have arrived. An integrated approach utilizing all tools available will be the clearest path to success in Total Quality. ●••

18

*Employee Training
And The Quality
Process*

Companies and their managements proclaim their commit-
ment to Total Quality and no doubt sincerely mean it. The problem is
that nearly all of the actual customer contact will take place at the lower
levels of the company—at the counters, on the sales floors, on the tail-
gate of a delivery truck, over the telephone from the accounting department.

The employees who staff these key positions come to their jobs generally with the best of intentions and a desire to represent the company well.
They look to management, however, to set the standards of performance
and to give specific guidelines on just how far they are to go in providing
extraordinary levels of service. If the talk of quality remains only at the
executive and managerial level then the whole program becomes somewhat of a farce.

The assimilation of workers into a quality culture must begin and be
continually reinforced by a well thought out, clearly defined training process which centers around the company's own quality policy, deals with
unique problems of the given industry, and incorporates basic concepts
common to all companies working on Total Quality.

The easiest part is laying out the initial orientation and training for
new employees. Because the employee has not actively assumed his or her
duties, the trainer generally has total control of the situation and there are
few outside demands to interrupt the trainee's attention. The greater chal-

lenge is developing a program of continuous training in quality which will keep workers focused and looking at the "big picture" their individual actions are collectively painting.

To examine training in the context of TQM, let's take a look at three companies that have established national reputations in this area. We will talk to human resource specialists at 1992 Malcolm Baldrige Award winner Ritz-Carlton Hotels and a vice president of Maritz Continuous Improvement Systems, a division of the leading national employee motivation and incentive company Maritz, Inc. We will also review training in quality at product manufacturer Panduit Corporation.

⊚ Quality Training at Ritz-Carlton

Throughout the Ritz-Carlton network of hotels, a highly structured and consistent program of employee education and reinforcement in quality is continually underway. It is broad in scope, appealing to the worker's own self-esteem, while getting down to such specifics as what words are to be spoken upon greeting guests and in what manner guests are to be directed to areas of the hotel (they are always to be escorted to their destination rather than merely given directions).

The motto, "We Are Ladies and Gentlemen Serving Ladies and Gentlemen," instantly tells the worker that his status is important and that expectations for his level of performance are high.

Kim Starr Rist and Kevin Richeson, human resource directors at the St. Louis Ritz-Carlton property, shared with me some of the specific techniques used throughout the chain to frame the employees' training experience. Rist pointed to the underlying philosophies as reflected in the motto, their "Three Steps of Service," a "Credo," and what they call "The Ritz-Carlton Basics," which is a twenty point statement of the basic service-related duties of all hotel employees. These guidelines serve as the framework for an intensive training process both in the initial days of employment and through repetitive reinforcement in daily routines, according to Richeson.

Employment at Ritz-Carlton begins with a two-day orientation focusing on philosophy, quality, and the "Credo" card which defines duty and commitment to the hotel's guests. A unique feature of this training is a "scavenger hunt" which sends the new trainees out for one hour to find specific people or places within the hotel and teaches them to fill out forms such as an "internal defect" form which reports on a problem and calls upon them to make a suggestion for resolving it. Employees can expect someone will get back to them within twenty-four hours regarding the situation and their suggestion. Following this the department trainer takes over for five to seven days and focuses on duties specific to the employee's own job.

The group which begins training together is encouraged to discuss their findings and observations and a "class reunion" is held on what is called "Day 21." At this time the trainees are asked "what was it like?" and whether their experiences were consistent with the training provided.

A final step in the formal training process in quality is the "certifying" of a new employee which must be accomplished within sixty days. This involves evaluation via written material, inspection of the employee's work, and observation by the department supervisor. Most new employees achieve certified status sooner than the sixty day limit, says Richeson. Once formal training has been completed the employee's education continues under the wing of a team leader and the training supervisor.

An important factor in maintaining quality standards at Ritz-Carlton is the uniformity of procedures and sharing of data and feedback from hotel to hotel. Networking of training supervisors is encouraged with periodic meetings of managers from the different hotels to compare notes and exchange ideas.

While variations on themes may be developed by the training departments at the various locations, training still comes back to "The Ritz Carlton Basics" as the foundation for employee behavior. In fact, all Ritz hotels around the world focus on the same "Basic of the Day" as well as a topic of the day and a featured department. The Basics encompass points such as continually identifying defects, maintaining immaculate uniforms, use of proper telephone etiquette, knowledge of emergency procedures, and being a positive ambassador of the hotel in and out of the workplace. Employees are encouraged to "own" any complaint received from a customer and act to remedy the problem. They are specifically empowered to resolve incidents of customer dissatisfaction and prevent reoccurrence.

Another program utilized at all hotels is a daily "quality line-up" which involves a daily meeting of each work area team to review problems and check that standards are being met.

In the training process Rist and Richeson see little difference between functional work groups (i.e. clerical, housekeeping, sales, etc.) when it comes to the ability to adapt to Total Quality, but they do feel that those individuals who cope well with change fit most easily into the quality process and reap the most benefits from training.

"Quality is integrated into every aspect of our operations," says Rist.

With the Baldrige Award as testimony, they must be succeeding.

● Quality Training at Maritz

As specialists in worker productivity, the people at Maritz would certainly be expected to have refined the art of training to a high degree. In fact they have developed a whole range of training programs for their own employees which continually target the quality process.

According to Vice President Tom Tener, the emphasis on quality begins on the first day of employment in their orientation program. Each of the various operating units has training programs specific to the nature of their business and the needs of their own workers and customers.

Quality training is ongoing at Maritz, says Tener, and is woven into many management and line-worker courses. These programs have specific titles such as "Promises, Promises" (a program devoted to customer service) and "Selection Interviewing" for managers and supervisors.

Written manuals and materials are used extensively in Maritz training programs as well as proven adult learning techniques to convey the need for quality and the means to achieve it. These include lectures, case studies, role playing and role rehearsals, structured experiences, and many other formats. Supervisors play a critical role in the quality education provided by the training department. Their role is to set expectations before a subordinate attends training and to reinforce the classroom learning when the individual returns to the workplace.

The first step in quality training is, of course, to select the right people in the first place. At Maritz, the quality process impacts strongly on hiring decisions. Questions that get to a "Quality of Service Orientation" are specifically asked in each interview.

"Our bias is that it's easier to hire people with this bent than to try to train someone without it," says Tener.

Tener agrees with Rist and Richeson that there seem to be no significant differences between functional employee groups when it comes to willingness or ability to adapt to Total Quality.

"We don't vary training techniques by job function for TQM any more than we would for any other set of skills," he says.

The answer to TQM does not lie in the classroom, says Tener, but in the day-to-day on-the-job environment. Accordingly, the company's supervisors are the driving forces behind improving and maintaining quality.

"We like to think that we specialize in delighting our clients today and tomorrow. We define quality as exceeding our clients' expectations."

Tener goes on to say that, while extremely important, training by itself is not the "be all and end all, guaranteed to cure all quality problems. Excellent training is only as excellent as the systems that recognize and reinforce desired behaviors. Company management must give at least as much . . . maybe more . . . attention to these systems as to training design and delivery. If they don't, the whole effort may end up looking much like a one-legged duck . . . lots of actions, lots of paddling, but only going around in circles!"

● Panduit Ties Training to Quality

Panduit Corporation, a leading manufacturer of products to tie, identify, terminate, and contain electrical and electronic wiring, has been involved in the "quality revolution" for many years. According to information provided by Vice President for Corporate Quality Assurance Arlie Thayer, the company's "Excellence Thru Quality" (ETQ) process helps to ensure that all employees are involved in total quality assurance as a team effort.

Customized training is provided in techniques such as statistical process control, closed loop corrective action, problem-solving teams, and design reviews. Salesmen and distributors receive quality training through regular education programs to ensure that people working in the field can assist customers with application of products.

As a manufacturer of product, training here differs in focus from that at Ritz-Carlton and Maritz, which are primarily service companies. While Panduit also has a large service component, its quality effort must begin with the manufacturing process and products are designed to meet applicable UL, CSA, military and international standards. Quality assurance tools developed by Deming, Juran, Crosby, and other consultants are taught throughout the company.

Training the designated facilitators of the quality process is the key to success because they are the individuals within the company who must lead and carry out the program, says Donald Kardux of Toledo-based Business Navigators, a quality consulting firm. Kardux differentiates between the quality leaders and regular supervisors who he says also must be brought into the process.

"Don't treat the regular supervisors as extraneous to the process," says Kardux. "Let them know they are vital to success."

Kardux describes the best prospects for successful quality training as being people with healthy relationships and stable families. Intelligence is not nearly so important. On the other hand self-centered individuals, those with weak egos (manifested as large egos), and people who have been damaged by previous authority figures will likely resist the change inherent in TQM.

Therefore, says Kardux, successful training in quality may depend to a certain degree upon effective hiring practices. Management has a tendency not to anticipate personnel needs but to hire in a panic. He urges companies to take a good look at what it is they are really looking for, with special attention to the goals of the quality plan.

We have here looked at training in quality as it is conducted at several large companies. Again, at small enterprises, management will have substantially more day-to-day contact with line workers. Lacking a separate training staff, it is incumbant upon owner/managers to familiarize themselves with techniques of quality training so that they can use this close contact to convey not only a passion for total quality and meeting customer expectations, but can help employees as they grapple with specific improvement projects and seek to orient daily procedures towards zero defects.

Quality is a commitment. It must be more than lip service. Making it a reality requires an effective and well-thought-out program for training new employees and reinforcing the strengths of existing workers. ●●•

19

The Brainstorming Session

Total Quality means taking a look at operations from a fresh perspective. It means stepping back and analyzing goals, objectives, and processes to ensure that all resources are keyed in to meeting customer expectations.

An effective means of starting that process (or helping it along) is for key employees involved in TQ or any process for which improvement is sought to step out of the daily grind and take a look at the big picture. Call it a "brainstorming session," "think tank," or "retreat," the purpose is to put people together without distractions to improve systems, relationships, or processes.

Oftentimes a Total Quality process is initiated at a company through just such a session. Sometimes it is run by an outside consultant or it may be under the guidance of top management, trained by such a consultant, or perhaps fresh from attendance at a special seminar. The regular use of such sessions becomes part of the ongoing quality process and helps to build team concepts within an organization.

"We use these kinds of meetings for one day or over a weekend," says Dave Draga who is vice president and general manager of Indiana Supply Corporation. "It depends upon the time of year and what we're hoping to accomplish at the meeting."

Draga says these planning sessions are combined with some recreational activities such as a cook-out or swimming to encourage interpersonal communication. An agenda is put together by top management which attempts to focus on visionary concepts and thought-provoking ideas.

"The purpose is to define where we are and where we want to be," says Draga.

Typically, outside sales people and key administrative supervisory personnel will attend these meetings. Efforts are made to keep fairly close to an agenda for time purposes, but periods are designated for open discussion.

"We try to make the meetings all-inclusive," says Draga. "The results of the meeting should be documented. The facilitators should have the group rank topics in priority and come up with a consensus as to major problems to be attacked."

Draga says that if the group selects the problems and agrees on solutions they are more likely to "buy-in" to the program. They will want it to be a success rather than a failure.

"We document these ideas on an easel," says Draga. "They are then taken off and put in written form and passed out to those in attendance. Items agreed upon are put on agendas for subsequent sales meetings."

Oftentimes a specific course of action for a department is set up as a result of these meetings. Draga separates the output of such a meeting into two categories:

1. *Issues that can be taken care of immediately— Here the company may have lost touch with a concept or taken something for granted. Eyes are opened by communication from people in other departments and action is taken immediately following the meeting.*

2. *Medium or longer-range issues— These need to have a little more time or may require input from people not at the meeting. Perhaps it may have come up as a good marketing idea but it would create internal havoc for the accounting department. The left side must consult with the right side before this idea can be instituted.*

Within the quality process, a more limited form of "brainstorming" might be utilized to attack a specific problem or process.

Jeff Holmes, quality control manager of Airguard Industries, Inc., the Louisville-based manufacturer of air filters, describes these "optimization" meetings held at the company's Indiana plant.

"We meet with customers and bring in key people off the production line and supervisors from the area as well as somebody from the quality, scheduling, and maintenance departments."

Holmes says these optimization meetings explore how to make a project better, at decreased costs. This is the reason the process is described as "optimizing."

"When we have a new product coming on line, we try to assemble a similar group to work out problems before production," says Holmes. "It's a lot easier to work on it at the theoretical stage. The role of the facilitator is rotated through management."

Agendas for the "optimization" sessions are set by the different managers involved, depending upon the emphasis of the meeting.

"We ask what is the project—who is the customer? A different person will generally be in charge each time," says Holmes. "If a person has been in charge of a project it makes them better at working for somebody else. Nothing makes a good leader like being a good follower."

Hourly and line employees at Airguard are paid for the time they spend at these meetings. This is a recognition that it's part of their job to help improve performance and is evidence of management support.

Holmes describes the meetings as fairly open-ended, using the traditional brainstorming approach similar to that described earlier at Indiana Supply. Again, a poster board or easel is used with product or process problems ranked in order. All ideas are listed, no matter how offbeat. Similar issues are grouped together and everyone ranks them in order of importance and consensus is developed as to what the top three to five problems are and these are the problems which are attacked first.

Holmes suggests working on problems that can be resolved quickly to encourage the group to deal with the tougher concerns.

"Get one small success under your belt and then go after the bigger ones," he says.

The optimization group summarizes their findings and then sends them along to the plant manager as well as to the people on the committee. The group then breaks up into subgroups to address components of the issues and to provide subsequent status reports.

Holmes says the optimization groups do not get all the issues resolved but they try to enact enough that everyone feels that headway has been made.

"As long as we're making progress or becoming a little better at what we do, we can say it's time well-spent," says Holmes.

With what frequency are meetings held? At Indiana Supply, they try to set them up at least once or twice a year. The company is currently working with a consultant on an integrated series of four such meetings. At Airguard, meetings are called when there is a specific problem or need. There is no set schedule of meetings.

"We do have a 'Product of the Quarter' emphasizing an item for everyone to focus on," says Holmes. "Whether we get to the optimization meeting stage depends on whether a problem exists or if there is a specific competitive situation we need to take a look at."

Stepping out of the established routine, taking a deep breath and looking at where you are going can help to keep a company focused on the quality process. Similar techniques can come up with solutions to problems which might otherwise repeat themselves or get caught up in inter-department squabbling or failed communication.

The "brainstorming session," by whatever term, is an important device to keep a company traveling down the road to quality. ●●•

20

Creativity In Quality

It is so easy for a business owner or a staffer at a large corporation to seize upon Total Quality as an answer to all problems. It comes as a nice, clean, pre-packaged program which promises solutions for all the company's ills.

Certainly there is no dearth of consultants and advisors willing to help you set course and there is a great abundance of written resource materials. If one follows the prevailing methodologies workers will soon be awash in statistical process control, suggestion forms, goal-setting criteria, and any number of formalized approaches to producing a better widget that will appeal to ever greater numbers of cutomers.

One of the criticisms most frequently leveled at TQM is that it often exhibits a great deal of sound and fury, signifying nothing. Workers may devote vast numbers of hours to training, team meetings, and interpersonal exercises with little real focus on business results.

In a world with ever tightening competition and ever more segmented markets, the entrepreneurial traits of creativity and imagination become all the more important. Recognizing and seizing opportunities, and developing efficient means of meeting those opportunities, must be talents encouraged by a quality process rather than inhibited.

The process must be approached from the creative side with emphasis on self-discovery, says Don Kardux.

"The group must figure out what's wrong and how they can make it better."

Indeed, the majority of programs out there are rigid, snug, and tightly structured, charges Dave Gleason of Systematic Selling, Inc. While the parameters of the quality process are the same for all companies, the specifics of the program (including the goals chosen) will not be the same for any two individuals or companies.

Total Quality programs are sometimes criticized as being too caught up in procedures to be really effective. Perhaps in some instances this is not all bad.

"In our case we thought we could benefit from some rigidity of process," says Leo Walsh of Ohio's Columbus Temperature Control. "Small businesses sometimes need structure and this is hard to do in the small business environment because of the close relationships between owners and employees."

Bob Irwin at Sverdrup Corporation expressed his feelings that goals, processes, procedures, and measures are all important to the Total Quality program but that they must be developed to fit the organization and culture in which they are applied.

"Many of our quality improvement projects are the result of creative ideas from employees," says Irwin.

He noted that the company had tried a suggestion system which initially did not generate much interest but, within the team framework of Total Quality, communication had opened up to the point where ideas began to flow freely.

A big part of encouraging this free flow of ideas is the inducement of top executives and managers to let go of their need to be all-knowing, and helping them develop the ability to admit they don't have all the answers. When they are able to approach workers in a non-defensive posture, sending a clear message that input is really desired, then ideas will begin to flow both ways. Individual workers and teams may make suggestions that stimulate "outside-the-box" thinking by managers used to analyzing problems and making decisions within traditional frameworks.

"When consistent forums are provided, then a suggestion box is not necessary since employees realize they have a vehicle for communication," says Kardux. "It is important that employees who come up with ideas and suggestions be properly recognized and gain visibility for their contributions. This can entail verbal praise or publication in a newsletter or any variety of means of calling attention to the achievement."

Kardux describes one particular company where a plaque is mounted over the site of a newly adopted process or improvement identifying it as "Bob's Suggestion" or some similar description.

At Brauer Supply in St. Louis, we have been blessed with a number of creative people through the years who have ventured out into areas that did not always clearly appear as the opportunities they turned out to be. Starting in the 1880's as a supplier of cast iron stove parts to people on the frontier west of the Mississippi, the company had to evolve with the times as heating stoves gave way to radiator heat, then forced air systems, and eventually air conditioning systems. Long before forced air heating became the norm Oscar Brauer, like his father August before him, made decisions to ride the wave of change, becoming the first distributor in the nation for the disposable air filter. In subsequent years William H. Brauer gambled successfully that he would find markets for thermal insulation and fastener product divisions. Recent years have seen us branch out into new geographic areas and new product markets. Time and resources are being devoted now with major suppliers to developing systems to promote indoor air quality and energy conservation.

The point to be made is not that creative change comes from one individual at the top of the organization, but that an atmosphere of seeking and promoting change and ideas must prevail if an organization is to survive over the long haul. All of the major directional changes at Brauer Supply cited above no doubt came from the thoughts, suggestions, and observations of the hundreds of people who have worked for the company over the century of its existence. The combined creativity of all resulted in a very changed, yet still prospering company, despite total disappearance of the market for the company's initial products.

Creativity need not stop at the plant gates. Bringing customers, vendors, and service organizations into the creative process can provide an interesting perspective and an objective pair of eyes to the company's efforts.

Walsh describes how at his company they put a message line on the invoices to the customers offering specific financial rewards for workable suggestions to improve service. While feedback was limited, it did send a clear message that the company was not only willing to listen to customers but was actively seeking their ideas.

It is helpful if employees are given the chance to "own" new processes and ideas. The quality teams can facilitate this by working to discover the truth in given problem areas and then management can assist them in getting help from quality professionals who can provide them with information about successful solutions developed at other companies. The team then can apply their own creativity to accepting, rejecting, or modifying proposed remedies to solve the problem.

"If you have a situation where workers 'own' a concept they will buy in to changes eighty per cent of the time," says Kardux, "otherwise you will only have an accceptance rate of around twenty-five per cent."

The typical description of a company which fosters creativity is the enterprise where failure is celebrated. The person who tries a new idea and falls on his face is lauded for having the courage and energy to try, thus encouraging that person and others around him to continue the process of seeking and defining new opportunities.

Unfortunately, in too many organizations, the worker-manager who takes the safe road and sticks with tried and true methods (even though they may be losing in the struggle against the competition) is the individual who, through attrition, rises to the top and leads his company down the road to mediocrity and oblivion.

It starts at the top!

Openness to new ideas and methods and willingness to devote the energy to experiment, coupled with the intestinal fortitude to accept failure and bounce back, are mandatory characteristics of an organization and its management that will survive and prosper.

Beyond the routine implementation of statistical control and procedures to prevent errors, a quality program must address this need! ●●•

21

Quality As A Culture

Much lip-service is given to the idea of creating a "quality culture" at a company.

What does this mean? And can one go in and literally change a culture which has been developed over many years?

The answers to these questions are not as straightforward as answers to some other problems with which we have dealt. Every company has a culture which may or may not be consistent with the public statements and goals espoused by management. This culture is a culmination of the company's history in the marketplace, the product or service industry in which they compete, the styles of the various owners and managers over the years, and is a synthesis of the separate personalities of the workers and managers presently making up the organization. The guiding ideology tends to come, again, from management and the goals, standards, and aspirations it has for the organization.

By commencing a Total Quality program, management is making an attempt to dramatically shift that culture towards a commitment to excellence and meeting customer expectations. For this to occur, quality must be at the forefront of everyone's thinking and symbols of that commitment must be evident throughout the organization.

"We started as a quality house," says Vice President Ken Urbanski of Detroit's Haber Operations. "We were always attempting to maintain high standards, but when we got involved with TQM it highlighted our deficiencies, gave us a chance to document them, and provided a method by which they could be remedied."

Total quality thus provides a framework around which to build quality structures where previously generalized efforts at meeting standards had to suffice.

Urbanski notes that while signs and charts can serve as visible symbols, a lot of the culture is built by one-on-one contacts with individual workers.

"If there is a rejected part, you go straight back to the individual who was responsible and involve him in the remedy," says Urbanski.

The positive side of problem resolution is continually played up. Much is expected from workers and examples of problems resolved are cited at production meetings and employee gatherings.

What does it mean to have a quality culture?

"For our purposes, it means being able to react on a consistent basis, giving customers what they want when they want it," says Urbanski.

He notes that many end users are going to "direct certification." This means they are not checking parts received at their plant, but are relying upon their supplier to provide consistent defect-free products.

"You can't have this without a quality culture!" says Urbanski.

A retreat from concepts of fault-finding and pinpointing blame is a key to a positive quality culture, says Leo Walsh of Columbus Temperature Control.

"The point is—what did we do? How can we do it better?" says Walsh.

A financial stake for employees in the success of the company, such as ownership by an ESOP, can be tied into the quality process.

"These kinds of programs go hand-in-glove with quality," says Walsh.

"If you talk about better lives for individuals within the company as a natural result of these efforts, eighty per cent of the people will commit to the process," says Don Kardux of Business Navigators. "Some people are selfish and cannot be easily changed, but the majority are well-intentioned."

Kardux says that it is incredible what happens to people's views of themselves and their organization if the company appeals to these good intentions. Pride in the company and a feeling that "I am the best" after they have demonstrated their ability to reach goals raises the self-esteem of everyone and creates a positive culture. There is a direct and exponential relationship between success in the initial stages of the quality process and positive change in the company culture.

Jo Ellen Lemmon of Parker-Kalon refers again to the use of symbols, citing the benefits of posters, charts, and visual reminders of the need to satisfy internal and external customers.

Customer complaints are posted in the Campbellsville, Kentucky, plant, says Lemmon, and are a constant reminder of the responsibility of everyone to prevent reoccurrence. Every manager at the plant has at least two "indicators" to chart so that specific progress can be targeted. Specific feedback is important. Managers and workers are looking to see if someone has noticed their progress or lack thereof. Employees will begin to focus on the process when they see results—when they do something and see that things have gotten better.

"You can chart all day long and tell them the process works, but until you can actually show them the improvement, you won't have complete acceptance," says Lemmon.

Part of the culture is an enhancement of employee self-esteem as people take increased pride in their work. Here the focus must be on the little things that lead to the big picture. Take housekeeping, for example. If a person's work area is clean they are likely to make better and more precise products. While we want things to happen overnight, we must begin chipping away at the little things that affect the whole.

Again, a quality culture demands that quality be at the forefront of everyone's thinking. Meetings must begin with attention to quality and managers must ensure that a substantial portion of their time is devoted to quality control as opposed to cost reduction and production speed.

Part of the growing culture can be a special language that develops. Part of this is internal within the company and may be derived from the program format of a particular consultant or quality guru. People may begin to speak in terms of "zero defect," "cost of quality," and similar phrases. The new language, or jargon, may result from participation in or programs imposed on a company by their customers' quality programs. Meeting criteria of customers' programs (which may be titled by a string of initials or some description of a rating system) becomes a part of the language used as managers and employees work to meet the customer specifications.

For an effective quality culture to take hold, there must be a passion for quality throughout the enterprise. This means an emotional commitment which goes beyond systems and procedures. The people in the company must really *WANT* to provide top-flight service. It must be important to them on a very basic level, totally separate from the collective financial benefits which might flow to everyone if the process is successful.

When everyone begins to feel this emotional commitment a true quality culture will have taken root. ●••

22

Hiring Quality Employees

You've got to have the right people!

All the good intentions in the world and all the motivational and training programs a company can devise will not overcome the attitude of the worker who has never learned to think in a quality, customer-oriented fashion.

Like any athletic program, good coaching can bring out the best in the players, but sometimes a championship can only be achieved by a combination of hard work, good coaching, and players with some degree of natural aptitude. Selecting those quality-inclined players for your team is an important step in building the company's quality culture.

Can you effectively screen new hires for adaptability to TQM?

Edward Andler, author of *Winning The Hiring Game*[1], says it is possible to screen new people and hire the right employees if you ask probing questions and then validate what the candidates tell you. "Validation is the key," says Andler, who is president of Certified Reference Checking in St. Louis. "People don't always fully understand their own strengths and weaknesses. Sometimes they really don't know how good or bad they are! People they have worked with may have a more objective view."

An example might be a candidate who stresses his leadership skills. An effective way of checking this is asking the candidate who you can speak with to verify this. Who has seen him in action?

"Any skill calls for a quality orientation," says Andler. "Attitude spells the difference in everything. When I tell a company that there are 'flat spots' in an applicant's qualifications, nine out of ten times it's attitude. A person can have all the ability in the world but if he has a bad attitude he will not succeed."

Andler says that one can see evidence of this all the time by looking at sports teams where highly talented players fail to produce because of their mental approach to the game and their teammates.

Andler suggests telling the candidate up front that you expect total honesty and that you will be checking references. Ask for the names of key players in the candidate's work life and have the candidate request that those people contact you. In this way, you avoid having to chase down references and you also learn something about the strength of his or her relationships if people will cooperate in helping a person land a job. Of course, you may want to call the references back after they contact you to verify their authenticity.

Dave Draga of Indiana Supply Corporation says it takes time and practice to develop skills in interviewing to identify those likely to succeed in a Total Quality process.

"Most people are not very good at knowing the sequence of questions to ask and most companies don't have specialists on staff. It comes over time and with proper education (such as attending seminars)."

Draga says the quality company will be looking for employees who demonstrate people skills, personality, good communication ability, and who give evidence of having a strong work ethic.

"These are warm fuzzies which are tough to evaluate," says Draga. "There are no guarantees. A smooth talker sometimes will not perform as well as he says he will."

Again, Andler urges thorough reference checking. "If they have a poor quality outlook and you talk to two or three people, you will find this out. It will be loud and clear if you are talking to a bad one."

Andler, who consults with businesses and presents seminars on hiring throughout the country, says the legal pitfalls of reference checking have been overstated. He urges employers to diligently go after the information.

"The law says: (1) You ask all people the same questions (i.e. women and minorities) and (2) Questions should be job related. These two rules should keep you out of trouble well over ninety-nine per cent of the time," says Andler.

Can you test effectively for quality? Draga says you can do this up to a point, but industry has not done a good job. Small businesses, in particular, need to use the resources available. These include commercial psychological testing services. Testing can be a confusing area. There are a lot of tests on the market that determine honesty but these are constantly changing and one has to evaluate what is available and its suitability for a given situation.

The quality company should be forthright in letting applicants know of the company's high standards. In all instances it is best to put everything on the table so there are no surprises later.

Tell them "We want people who take pride in their work."

Candidates are told that Indiana Supply is active in the quality improvement process, says Draga, and the interviewer then lays out some of the company goals.

Andler stresses that if it is standard practice for all employees to sign a "commitment to quality" or other such statement that this should also be made known to the new hires. Expanding on this concept of being forthright and honest about what is to come, Andler compares it to a recent experience he had as he prepared to join a group of anglers heading for a fishing trip in Canada.

"They explained that we were going to be doing some serious fishing, working hard, and that accommodations might be pretty rough. I was prepared for this and therefore was a better participant," he said. "It's the same way with letting a job applicant know what can be expected."

The new employee should be offered the opportunity to jump right into the quality process. If he or she has been properly prepared and you have selected wisely the employee will welcome this opportunity.

We have talked a lot about the development of a quality culture. New employees always bring with them a little of the culture of the previous employer. If the company he or she is leaving was deep into the quality process part of that spirit and enthusiasm might come with the new employee. If a person thinks quality and service this is a strength they will bring to their peers at the new job.

Draga agrees that TQ is interchangeable from company to company.

A lot of this is simply having a good understanding of the importance of understanding customer wants and needs and even companies without a Total Quality program may be strong in this area. He stresses the importance of having a good "farm system," however, and not relying on other companies to train your future workers.

In selecting among applicants, does experience in a TQ company give an employee an edge . . . and should it?

"I would say that it certainly wouldn't hurt," says Draga. "You can assume that he or she is that much farther ahead in understanding quality concepts and has probably already bought into a quality culture. He or she must be a believer, however, and must not be cynical as a result of exposure to a poorly run program."

Andler says quality cultures can vary among departments within a large company. He cites his experience as personnel manager at a multi-product plant. He recalls moving employees from department to department and sometimes good employees would be a bad fit. People or supervisor's standards varied from department to department and this is always likely to be the case in large companies.

"If the person is used to doing things on a quality basis they'll do well," says Andler. "If not, it will be a hard adjustment."

What if the quality program at a person's previous employer had a different orientation or methodology from his new work place?

"Diversity is a good thing," says Draga. "You need cheerleader types as well as statistically based people. You don't want a bunch of clones."

Andler summarizes his approach to hiring quality people in terms of an eighty-twenty rule. "Eighty per cent of your problems will come from twenty per cent of the people you hire. With a little bit of reference checking you can find out into which group the applicant falls."

Take the time to check that new hire out! Starting with the right people gives you a head start in the race for quality. ●●•

23

Problem-Solving In The Quality Process

f we didn't have any problems, we wouldn't have any business!

That should be a comforting thought to anyone struggling through daily efforts to resolve disputes, variances, and failure to meet customer expectations. How well and how quickly these problems are solved, as much as how infrequently they can be made to occur as a per cent of total activity, is a measure of the effectiveness of a company's TQM process. While the ideal is a preventive program that ensures no defects ever occur, the reality is that some will and problem-solving which is directed to correction or improvement of a process is far preferable to putting out fires or using a band-aid approach.

Can the quality process be used to attack specific problems or is it suitable only as an over-all preventive program?

Dave Draga at Indiana Supply in Indianapolis says it can be used for both purposes.

"We target in on specific problems. We find that by making people more aware of everything they do as a result of TQ, problems begin to take care of themselves."

Recurring problems can be looked at as "missed opportunities." If a problem keeps coming up again and again and departments seem to be taking pot shots at one another they know the problem must be addressed in a formalized way. Some problems may not be readily recognizable as the same issue because people view things from different angles.

"Everyone gets comfortable with the way they are doing things and tends not to think of irregularities as system problems," says Draga. "We really stress meeting internal customers' needs and this means looking at procedures that might be causing unnecessary problems."

New York consultant Dave Gleason of Systematic Selling, Inc., says one of the most effective ways to solve problems within an organization is by the use of groups. People are at the base of most problems, says Gleason, so get the people who must deal with the results of the problem involved in coming up with solutions. This should begin with breaking down the reasons for the problem and, once the causes are identified, making recommendations to eliminate or circumvent those causes.

At Airguard Industries, Inc., in Louisville, Quality Manager Jeff Holmes says there are certain areas the company keeps track of because they know they have had problems there in the past. If something pops up they will call together the production supervisors to look at the problem and begin to eliminate the things that have not caused the problem. The effort is focused on finding the root cause.

Holmes says they use the Ishikawa Diagram technique to narrow down a problem. Kaoru Ishikawa, one of the major quality gurus, uses a fishbone diagram with the head of the fish representing the end result. The lines of the skeleton are followed to analyze the various components of the process one by one.[1]

If you open up the definition of quality, says Holmes, you can break just about everything down in this fashion. It shouldn't be a personal thing. If you take too much of a human approach you end up blaming people and not situations.

"No one likes to have their work criticized," says Holmes. "Make it impersonal and analytical, focusing on the facts."

It's been said that there is a "quality solution" to every business problem. At the heart of every problem is some deficiency in quality. This may not be what people want to hear because it ultimately does point the finger at some lapse in someone's efforts or capability.

"A little bit of pride and ego have to be swallowed to get to the root of problems," says Draga. "Sometimes you just have to go back to the drawing board."

Do problems necessarily require that a consensus be reached?

According to Holmes, things do work better when everyone "buys in" to the solution, but he says there will be times when not everyone is happy. In these cases, supervisors must be skilled in gaining cooperation of those who disagree. We might say something such as, "Maybe this is not what you would have proposed, but it's worth a try. If it doesn't work we'll try a different angle."

Conflict or difference of opinion can be positive. It can bring out varied approaches to a problem and result in an airing of needed information. As long as these differences are just different ideas about how changes can or should be made it has a positive effect. The more resources for ideas you have, the more angles you have from which to attack the problem.

Gleason sees an additional benefit of conflict in that it makes it possible for management to ask for compromise and thus gain support from all parties for the solution which is finally hammered out.

The Total Quality company will marshal all those resources in a non-adversarial way to come up with the best resolution to conflict and problems. ●●•

24

Quality And The Sales Process

Since time immemorial sales people have been subjected to motivational speeches, pep rallies, and any number of programs designed to push them to excel. Is it not then strange that somehow the selling process has been de-emphasized in most people's understanding of Total Quality Management?

"Part of the problem is that the quality improvement process developed from a manufacturing standpoint," says consultant Dave Gleason. "It was not developed for the service industry and did not initially deal with any aspect of selling."

The most visible sign of the sales department's involvement is generally in actively trumpeting the fact that a quality process exists at a company and how it will benefit the customer.

"Quality" by its very name evokes thoughts of a manufactured product or a defect-free procedure and, therefore, statistical measurements, self-directed teams and other facets of TQM tend to be focused on non-sales actvities. Of course, in a sales organization, all of these could be said to be sales related. But the actual one-on-one persuasion of the customer is somehow viewed as set and apart from the quality aspects of a company's operation.

Is not a successful communicating of the value to be added to a product by a company's unique service the first quality contact experienced by the customer?

This concept of value-added selling is given much lip service in trade periodicals and by sales force managers. Nevertheless, in company after company and industry after industry (despite the expanding quality movement) profit margins are eroding as competitors chase elusive market shares at all cost.

Does Total Quality provide an alternative to the ever-continuing auction selling which characterizes competition today?

"If you are asking your people to put more quality into their products and services then you must charge more," says Chuck Reaves, well-known consultant and speaker on sales topics. Reaves was at one time the top sales person for AT & T before becoming sales manager and then departing to form his own consulting company.

"People are willing to pay for quality so the successful sales person must go out and sell that quality," says Reaves. "If an organization is asking its people to sell value-added, then it has the responsibility to deliver quality products and services."

The sales person's role is to change the customer's perception of him from an order-taker to a problem-solver. When he shows up at the customer's door he or she must send the clear message "I'm here to help." This means being a good listener and viewing things from the customer's point of view.

Reaves suggests that on each sales call the representative should try to define the top three problems facing the customer and try to find some remedy which can be brought about by the products or services he has to offer.

Defining these problems and developing solutions means refining the art of asking questions. In commodity selling, according to Reaves, we've been taught to know answers. In value-added selling we are not selling what a product is, rather we are selling what it does for the customer. He suggests asking the same question several times, phrased in a different manner, and focusing on the final answer given by the customer to ascertain just what are the person's needs.

Opening questions, says Reaves, should not have anything to do with the salesperson's product, service, or company. This technique of questioning involves the customer in the process of problem resolution and makes solutions agreed upon a result of joint effort. Initial questioning will generally produce only symptoms of the problem which is why the constant rephrasing should be employed until the heart of the matter is reached. The whole focus here is on discovering the customer's real needs, not just his or her perceived needs. Once this is uncovered the value-added salesperson will highlight the need and focus on solutions rather than the price of the products he or she is selling. This verifies the need and gives a customer a reason to act.

A company's commitment to quality, if properly communicated to its customer base, will help to move the discussion away from price since the quality company's true goal is to make partners of its customers and the charging and receiving of a "fair" price will be accepted as something naturally flowing from that partnership.

"On the lower levels of value-added selling we learn to overcome price objections. On higher levels we learn to eliminate it and as we get farther into the concept we talk less and less and listen more," says Reaves.

In many ways sales people and organizations who focus on value-added selling are engaging in activity synonomous with Total Quality.

The salesman focusing on the value-added concept sells himself as a part of that value. He "comes with the sale" and becomes a sort of consultant to the purchaser, helping to sell and explain concepts to other parties within the purchaser's organization. He becomes a partner in the buyer company's own quality process, be it de facto or formalized. By his efforts, the salesperson brings about a perception on the part of the buyer that the products or services offered (along with the salesman and his company) are of greater value than the price being charged.

This, says Reaves, removes the objection to price because this objection arises when the customer does not perceive there is value in what is being offered. The salesperson ensures that the perception of quality is there and then has a responsibility to provide feedback and encouragement to the rest of the company to make sure that quality is a reality after the order is placed.

Reaves says the successful value-added companies have a passion for quality in all areas and an intensity for quality in specific areas. Quality in these organizations is at the forefront of thinking in all departments, functions, and individuals. An offshoot of this is a quick response to any threat from a competitor where a loss of business raises questions as to whether it has resulted from a weakness in the company and, once identified, whether steps can be taken to provide a solution.

It all comes down to communicating with the customer, and this must be two-way communication.

"If you don't work on developing relationships your sales will fall off," says Gleason. "You must make sure that the customer is heard and feedback flows back and forth. The salesperson is the conduit for this information."

Gleason is quick to point out that quality encompasses many areas, from person-to-person or relationship selling to cost control of a representative's sales calls to the concise reporting of information for market analysis. Not the least of these focuses is the consistent planning and carrying out of quality sales calls, which, according to Gleason, revolve around the following:

1. The salesperson must pre-plan what will happen on the call.

2. The customer will react and the salesperson must listen and then take care of the customer's needs while still achieving the objective of the call.

When a company initiates a formal quality process the sales force, always the closest to the customers, can take the lead in communicating the necessity for meeting customer expectations to the general employee group. While thinking of their actions in terms of impact on the ultimate customers may be a strange and unfamiliar exercise to auditors, accountants, and maintenance staff, the sales representatives can help to effectively translate the imperative nature of this need. Where once this strange preoccupation with doing everything "perfectly" may have rankled internal workers who saw special efforts on behalf of a customer as merely disrupting smooth running systems, special efforts above and beyond the call of duty to meet that customer emergency can become a common effort from which all can take satisfaction.

The sales force, if properly motivated and not anchored down by years of bad habits, can be a core group around which successful quality programs can be built. A smoothly functioning organization, focusing on customer needs and dedicated to zero customer defects, can be the ultimate value-added feature to give the sales representative a competitive edge. ●●•

25

Leadership And The Quality Process

The one thing that comes through again and again when one talks with quality managers and consultants is the importance of leadership—commitment from the top of the organization, demonstrated at the inception of a program and characterized by follow-through over a long period of time.

The ideal leader suited for TQM therefore would possess both the charisma to lead the charge in the opening days of the program and the "bean-counter" skills to monitor and follow up on statistical results. He or she will need to have a total conviction that the process is valid and worthwhile because skepticism on the part of employees is naturally to be expected. This is true especially if management of the company has pursued other "fads" in management style which have fallen by the wayside.

Leadership is, however, required at all levels to make the program work. Supervisors and foremen, particularly, need to set and demand standards of performance in customer contact matters and in matters of production quality. Their commitment is very visible to the line employees and therefore a goodly percentage of the training dollars should be invested in these key people. They must feel "ownership" of the process along with top management. This means that the general manager or CEO must be careful not to give the impression that quality is a one-person crusade but rather that it is a team goal involving the entire company as players.

All this aside, a great deal of the success or failure does rest with the chief executive of the company because managers and supervisors on down the line will take their cue from his level of commitment and his passion for meeting customer expectations.

"The company president must continue to put emphasis behind the quality process," says Ken Sisson, who fills that post at Mid-Way Supply in Zion, Illinois, just north of Chicago. "He must make sure that enthusiasm for the new process does not die."

Sisson notes that the company CEO should interact regularly with the quality steering committee or action teams. At his company, recommendations from quality action teams are delivered to the president's office on at least a quarterly basis.

"The president is the one everyone watches to see if procedures and policies are being followed," says Jo Ellenn Lemmon of Parker-Kalon. "People say 'What are they doing that lets me know I am their internal customer?'"

Top management needs to be right in there pitching with everyone else.

Jerry Peterson of Mortemp, Inc. in Seattle feels that the CEO must be chairman of the quality process to ensure that workers and managers know the importance attached to it.

"The CEO has to be the leader of the effort or the QI system won't fly," says Bill Beck, vice president of Precisionaire Inc., in St. Petersburg, Florida.

Beck recalls one of his vendors who put a lot of money into a quality process without proper leadership from the top. The program quickly died but was brought back after a period of time with new leadership in the company and it is working well.

Beck argues that seventy-five per cent of the credit or blame for success or failure belongs to top management. Beyond this level, leaders and facilitators must be selected as well as steering committee members. Many large companies have a separate officer or manager designated as leader of the quality process. It is generally best if this person has an overall idea of what the business is about and that he or she is not heavily tied to any one department, such as manufacturing. He or she must not show preference to any one department or have any axes to grind. The facilitator must be able to attack quality problems as the pure problems they are without need to protect anyone's ego and without raising defensive reactions from those with whom he's dealing.

What are the ideal characteristics of leadership in a TQM program?

"The people chosen to lead must be committed to persistence," says Sisson. "They must realize they are only dealing with a small slice of the company at any one time."

These chosen leaders must have the personality strength to risk ridicule from those workers who are apt to deride all the effort as a silly waste of time. This will happen and the leaders must display such strong conviction and faith in the process that skeptical employees will at least give the process a reasonable chance to develop and get past the initial stages.

Formalized training for leaders of teams (these are separate and distinct from steering committees) is important.

"We set up in-house training programs," says Beck. "We've brought people into Precisionaire who have taught our team leaders and first level supervisors."

Beck notes that project teams begin at the management level. Middle managers have become involved and finally the program has been focused down to the employees. Leadership of the teams has passed in a progression from team member to team leader, and employees at all levels have the opportunity to assume leadership roles.

In the following chapter, Peter Schutz argues that decision-making should be done democratically and carried out dictatorially. Does this same reasoning apply to leadership in the quality process?

Most quality managers I have spoken with lean toward participatory methods in this process.

Arguing strongly for a democratic process in TQM, Jo Ellen Lemmon of Parker-Kalon says, "We've found most programs work better if everyone feels they have a say in decisions as opposed to having procedures imposed upon them autocratically. In the absence of this kind of input employees tend to react to new policies and procedures with skepticism and a sense of 'O.K., here comes something from on high.'"

Must the quality facilitator be relatively free from other responsibilities? Does leadership of the process require an individual's full time?

A small business cannot afford the luxury of a full-time coordinator. In some sense, anyway, a full-time quality person might be so far removed from daily customer contact that he or she would be unable to develop and implement a realistic program or perhaps the employees would be reluctant to follow such a manager in the quality process because of his or her lack of credibility since he or she has no active involvement in the competitive wars in which the workers are engaged. Recognizing this, the most effective quality manager will likely have other major responsibilities within the company, but it is important that the message comes through loud and clear that "quality is number one" in that individual's priorities. He or she must never do anything that sends a message that expediency or saving a buck takes precedence over quality. He or she must exhibit an intolerance for defective products or services which should become contagious throughout the organization if the process is really taking hold.

With other major responsibilities within the company there is a temptation to place quality on the back burner and take care of what seems to be more pressing needs. Time and again this is the reason given by managers I speak with as to why their quality program is running out of steam. They just don't have time!

An honest analysis of the cost of quality will tell us, of course, that we don't have time because we are putting out fires due to quality-related problems. With attention focused initially on quality those problems should largely evaporate and free up additional management time.

Leaders in the process must continue to take the long-range view. They must be convinced that the hours spent in checking, training, and determining and meeting customer expectations will have a pay-back in smoother operations and profitable performance which will justify the efforts put forth. ●●•

26

Quality And The Decision Making Process

Why is it necessary to "manage?"

Peter W. Schutz, former CEO of Porsche AG Worldwide, answers that question succinctly in one word—Change!"

Schutz is the American engineer who progressed from executive positions at Caterpillar Tractor and Cummins Engine Company to serve from 1981 through 1987 in the top position at Porsche, a period which showed substantial success for that company and which provided him with a source of rich examples relating to his management philosophy.

Having developed his theories from contact with the many people with whom he came in contact during his management years, Schutz now consults with growing businesses and major corporations at lectures on management techniques in the United States and Europe.

Schutz declares that every time there is any change, inside or outside of the business, there is an immediate need to (1) decide what to do, or what not to do and then (2) get it done! Implement!

The more change there is, the more there is a need for professional management, and the more the penalty for poor management escalates.

The decision-making process can and should be a democratic process, according to Schutz, with input sought from all those who may be affected by the decision. Those to be affected will ultimately have power over the successful implementation and therefore their diverse interests must be accommodated in arriving at a workable decision. Once the decision is made, however, implementation becomes a dictatorial process. Where companies get into trouble, Schutz says, is when they get this process backwards. Where the decision is made by one person at the top followed by everyone getting their "two cents" in, the policy begins to dissipate as employees comply or do not comply with the edict.

If the process is followed correctly, it becomes easy to predict the ultimate quality of a decision. With decisions made democratically, management will have the support of the diverse interests on whom they depend for implementation and can proceed with confidence that a policy will be carried out.

"A quality decison must satisfy four dimensions," says Schutz. "If any one dimension is not adequately covered, mismanagement will result!" He lists these four dimensions as (1) *Producing Results*–making money by adding value with the value being defined by the customer. (2) *Administration*–organizing and systematizing via procedures. (3) *Entrepreneurial*–This is the skill of repositioning the business when external factors change (competition, environment, strengths and weaknesses). This is the "vision" aspect of management. (4)*Integration*–This is the concept of an enterprise functioning similar to a family with commitment to each other and to a shared set of values.

In simpler days, dimensions one and two (producing results and administration) were generally sufficient for business survival. With the volatile economy we now face, there is far more emphasis on dimensions three and four. Businesses are called upon to take risks and change positions rapidly due to the rapidly changing technology brought about by computers and other high tech developments.

An example cited by Schutz is the change undertaken by some record and phonograph companies that were faced with the advent of the laser disc. It is easy to imagine that any industry could be faced overnight with a new development that could make obsolete virtually every product they made or had previously sold. The successful companies anticipate these changes and risk (a risk which is not insubstantial) of repositioning themselves for survival.

It is important to note that businesses cannot rely on their customers to tell them when this repositioning is needed. The customer base as a whole will not be that far ahead on technology and so the manufacturer/distributor must anticipate these changes. This means keeping up to date on current literature and trade periodicals, attending trade shows, and maintaining a well-established network of associates in the industry.

The fourth dimension, integration, becomes increasingly important because it encourages companies to take long-term views of their market-place and bypass the temptation to grab for quick profits which may not be in the company's long-term interest.

Family businesses can be uniquely gifted in this area since, at least if there is cohesiveness and shared values in the family, the emphasis oftentimes is on preservation from one generation to the next rather than short-term profits. Managers, as members of the family, may also see their long-term success tied to perpetuity of the enterprise rather than plus or minus profit figures for the upcoming quarter.

With respect to corporate structure, Schutz stresses the flexibility of organizations which place complete responsiblity for a given market (i.e., either product or geographical) in one chief operating officer who is held responsible for the outcome of sales, production, administration, and personnel. Task forces to achieve specific short-term goals should come out of the operating units so that there is cohesiveness and so that the chief operating officer of that unit is able to draw on the shared commitment of his group.

It is important to keep control of an operation without letting administrative procedures run the company. Middle managers should be constantly reminded that their chief job is to make the sales and production efforts of the company as easy as possible for mission workers charged with carrying out those functions.

Schutz warns against management by manipulation. The most dangerous managers are those manipulators so clever that the people being manipulated feel motivated. These managers are often hailed as miracle workers because they can turn out large sales increases or increases in profit in the short term. At some point, however, they are found out by someone within the organization who then spills the beans that the workers and managers are being exploited, and at that point everything generally comes to a halt. Such "miracle workers" then generally move on to other organizations to repeat the process until word gets around and they are no longer able to effectively repeat the scenario.

To get things done within an organization we need to ensure that those with the legal right to decide on matters of "yes" and "no" also have the true authority to make that decision. It is not uncommon for organizations to have people who titularly have authority but know they must check with the owners or some other person before they can truly proceed.

Who has power in the business? Whoever we depend on for cooperation to get things done! If we could do it alone we would not need an organization. Rather than manipulating people, we must use influence to persuade others to do what we want done because it is truly in their interest to do so. This is the essence of motivation.

Applying these theories to quality programs in general, Schutz says, "To be successful, the program must have staying power, and for that to happen the people implementing the program must be sure they have satisfied all diverse interests who can make or break the program!" ●●•

27

Quality And Technology

The office and plant of the twenty-first century will be a far different place than we see today. According to technology consultants, changes are waiting in the wings that will continue to enhance our ability to work faster and more accurately. It's not hard to accept this because recent years have seen a transformation of the work processes that were taken for granted for decades.

New technology seems destined to usher in still more productivity and efficiency . . . or will it? What limitations are there on people's ability to keep up with technology? What does a Total Quality orientation have to offer to ease this transition? What does this mean for TQM's emphasis on human interaction and worker empowerment?

"That's a danger," says Reell Precision Manufacturing's Steve Wikstrom in St. Paul. "I remember reading that Toyota spoke of 'automation with a human touch'. The question is how do we use automation in a way that is complementary to people? Machines and people must interact."

We must not become too comfortable with the amenities of technology, says Maritz Motivation's Tom Tener.

"I stepped out into the office one day and everyone's head was down in their PC," he said. "Granted, you can't get the job done today without such things as personal computers and voice mail, but these must be managed. It doesn't help if people hide behind voice mail to screen calls or if technology is used to avoid human interaction."

Tener warns that technology should be directed to making things easier for the client, not just the worker. It's easy, for example, to put a telephone on "Do Not Disturb," but this does not help the client/customer who is trying to get hold of his sales representative and in the long run it's not good for that employee or his company.

From the standpoint of job creation, there can be a long-term benefit if the company uses technology to grow because new kinds of jobs will be available even though more automation will reduce the numbers of jobs for a given process. The key thing is that technology use must indeed improve a company's position and must be related to meeting customer needs.

Should the quality company be out in front with technology or wait until it is perfected? Does moving too far in front of the pack create risks of outstripping worker capabilities to keep up and retain a customer focus?

"You don't have any choice if you are perceived as a quality company," says Wikstrom. "You will be drawn to be out on the leading edge because you will be standing apart from the competition. The customers will seek you out and involve your company in the earlier stages to talk more about their needs."

Larry Miller, president of Superior Supply in Kansas City, says the quality company should be at the forefront of new technology.

"Quality is a perception," says Miller. "It means being a leader in the industry and utilization of new technology helps give the customer confidence in a company."

Quality Manager Mike Berry of Southwestern Bell Telephone says that a company with strong Total Quality can take better advantage of new technology because their people understand their processes better and what impact it will have. If the process is messed up, better technology will likely only compound the problem. If a process is wasting raw materials, technology may only allow that company to make scrap faster.

Oftentimes there is a tendency for companies to substitute technology for quality customer service. The thought is, "If we spend all this money, surely we'll get better!" But technology is only a part of a Total Quality effort.

A company could dig itself into a hole by relying on technology to solve all problems. There is no panacea and new high tech equipment will be a wasted resource if an organization is not disciplined and the people are not prepared to do a day's work in a day's time.

"The quality company won't ignore the customer as processes are enhanced," says Precisionaire's Bill Beck. "You will take care of him in more effective ways. You cannot isolate on the technology itself. You must spend money on both ends...equipment and people."

The big problem is balance, agrees Wikstrom. It's relatively easy to get good at serving any one constituency, but you must continue to improve in serving all of them. Customer service and technology must go hand in hand. You cannot abandon one as you concentrate on the other. This, says Wikstrom, is the real challenge.

What is the impact of rapidly changing technology on the workers themselves?

"Rapid change in an atmosphere of pressure and little control breaks down the morale of workers," says psychologist Patrick Openlander. "There is a necessary ratio between challenge and support. Too much challenge at too fast a pace can overwhelm anyone!"

Openlander, who has served on the faculties of Washington University and St. Louis University and currently operates a private counseling service, says that the onslaught of technological change without integration can produce fatigue, irritability, and discouragement. Worn out workers and supervisors make mistakes, argue, and have lower productivity.

"Workers resent change which is not explained well, which does not appear comprehensible in terms of larger organizational goals, and which is not related to being more competitive," says Openlander. "Even well-trained and highly motivated workers can be expected to complain initially when technological changes are introduced. When they feel cut off from the reasons for change, they simply will not respond energetically or enthusiastically."

According to Openlander, the atmosphere of support and information sharing which is inherent in the Total Quality process is essential for coping with rapid change. Workers who make commitments to their employer frequently want the chance to renew their skills and understand that familiarity with cutting edge ideas and technology is their guarantee of stable employment.

"With coaching and involvement with supervisors and with team concepts that are real, workers can overcome anxiety about change and embrace it," says Openlander. "TQM builds confidence in and ownership of change."

Openlander says the best way to keep productivity growing and employment stable is to keep workers informed and involved. Work that evolves, becomes more efficient, and permits workers to give input will typically mean a setting that attracts people. A Total Quality program can help create just such a setting.

Is there a risk of technology becoming a goal unto itself? How do we make it our servant and not our master?

Beck says it is important that we not lose track of where we are going with our customers. There is a give and take from both ends and if a new computer system doesn't improve customer service, for example, it is basically worthless. It must have a value in what the company is doing and any improvement must focus on improving things for the customer.

"Don't just look for a better computer system without asking what it will do for the customer," says Beck.

Wikstrom suggests making a clear statement that technology must be designed to serve the company's objectives.

"I remember when we designed our first computer system," says Wikstrom. "We sat around a table and committed to make the machine do what we wanted it to do. This meant we had to be prepared to spend the money for additional software enhancements to conform the system to our needs and those of our customers, not just accepting what the system was prepared to do in its initial state."

Technology is a tool to be used to help a company get where it intends to go in a faster and more efficient way, but investment in technology must be matched with investment in people and training or dollars spent on hardware and machines will be wasted.

The workforce must be comfortable with the tools they are given and this means not only education, but making sure workers understand how it all fits into company goals and strategic plans and what their individual roles are in these plans.

Cutting edge technology? Yes, the TQ company will be there, but it will be only a part of an integrated approach to constant improvement. Management must first ask how the new device will make things easier for the customers to do business with the company. If there is no answer to that question then resources might best be allocated elsewhere! ●●•

28

Accuracy In The Quality Process

I t's easy to sell anybody the first time! The profitable company needs the fourth, fifth, and sixth sale to begin to really build a base.

This repeat business, the backbone of selling, comes about because of the customer's confidence earned by the company's ability to deliver quality, defect-free service and products.

"We verify accuracy because we know the product we put out the door is held up for scrutiny by our customers," says Sales Manager Jay Hepler of A-1 Compressor, Inc., in Indianapolis. "If we don't produce defect-free products we open the door for people to suspect our product's ability to perform, affecting our ultimate goal of getting repeat business."

This emphasis on accuracy in product or service delivery is an important component of the quality process and is approached in numerous ways by manufacturers, sales organizations, and professional service firms.

Manufacturers establish standards which are reviewed by management and quality teams. These take the form of tolerance specifications for the manufactured product.

"Tolerance specifications are given to each job station for each type of product we make," says Hepler. "These are spot-checked by supervisors to ensure product is falling within this range. Every operation is signed off so that we know what person was responsible for each aspect. Supervisors sign off indicating that they have provided an additional round of checking."

121

All facets of the operation at A-1 are subjected to the checking procedure. This includes parts which are reviewed and signed off for before they reach the assembly area. The receiving department also works with quality control when new parts or material are received and these new items are subjected to a separate quality audit. The audit is either a 100 per cent checking process or a sampling, depending upon previous experience with the given supplier.

President Larry Miller of Kansas City's Superior Supply Company recognizes that accuracy in a sales and service business is a reflection of customer satisfaction.

"Our primary check on accuracy is customer feedback," says Miller. "We judge how well we're doing by the number of complaints we receive from the field. If we start hearing of a problem we attack it immediately. We try to create a culture where this immediate response is expected from every employee."

Miller notes that in a small company such as his it is easy to fix responsibility.

"We keep track of back orders and lost sales opportunities so we can improve our inventory levels and ordering ability," says Miller. "We keep records manually and then log them into the computer so that we create a data base to highlight and investigate problems."

In line with this emphasis on customer feedback, Miller has established an 800 number for customers to call management directly if a service problem arises. They also use surveys with postage paid reply cards to keep the lines of communication open.

As in the manufacturing process, the rendering of professional services places a premium on accuracy and reliability. When engineers, lawyers, or doctors render advice or services, customers expect to be able to rely on the precision of their work and great consequences ride on the quality of their product.

At Kuether and Associates, Inc., a national engineering firm specializing in electric utility transmission and distribution design, Regional Vice President and Manager of Engineering Richard Mues outlines the four reasons why accuracy is essential in this kind of enterprise. These reasons are:

1. TO MAINTAIN THE EXISTING CLIENT BASE. *"Cost and schedule problems can be overcome," says Mues, "but not substandard quality."*

2. **LEGAL REASONS.** *The professional services firm must maintain some kind of errors and omissions or professional liability insurance and poor quality will soon be reflected in this major expense.*

3. **SCOPE OF POTENTIAL LOSS.** *If there is a failure in a structure or foundation the loss in dollars and property can be great.*

4. **PUBLIC SAFETY.** *This is paramount in all such projects.*

As part of the company's quality program, Mues recently developed a "Quality Control and Checking Procedure" which is distributed to all of the firm's employees and given to clients as a business development tool.

"We require every employee to read this policy annually and sign off a statement saying they have read and understand it," says Mues. "Many engineering firms have a similar statement but each develops their individual language."

The procedure at Kuether calls for review of all calculations, drawings, and specifications, with an assigned engineer or designer for each task and a separate assigned person to check the work product. After the initial checking it must be reviewed by a professional engineer who is registered in whatever discipline may be involved (i.e., electrical, civil, or structural).

"The person who does this review is not part of the project team so he is not biased," says Mues. "He is totally independent and looks to see if the project is engineered and designed in conformance with standard practices, whether it meets codes and would meet customer requirements, and whether or not an experienced engineer would come to the same conclusions."

Following the engineer's review, the project manager conducts what is termed a "project adequacy check" to see if the work meets all the requirements of the contract and whether anything has been left out.

How is it determined who will verify each step? Mues says the person with the most experience in a given type of work is assigned to a similar job and the goal is to have the skill of the checker exceed that of the person preparing the work. If a project engineer does not feel a step in the checking procedure is needed only the CEO can authorize its omission.

With TQM's emphsis on meeting customer expectations, what role does the customer play in verifying professional work?

"Clients are involved, but not responsible," says Mues. "In a typical project, drawings will be sent to the client for review and comment at thirty, sixty, and ninety per cent completion. At one-hundred per cent the client's approval is sought, but this does not relieve the engineering firm of responsibility."

Industries establish standards which, in effect, are a form of quality control. In Kuether's case, they must comply with the National Electrical Safety Code, part of the American National Standard (ANSI). Other professions may have standards established by trade associations and state licensing boards.

Does the computer come into use in accuracy verification?

"In a way it does," says Mues. "When a new computer program is developed it must go through the same checking procedure so that in the future they need only check the input data because the program has already been extensively reviewed."

The initial cost of accuracy verification can be somewhat expensive, but all seem to agree that the long-term costs of correcting defects and dealing with customer ill will is far greater.

"It's more cost-effective for us to do things right the first time than to go back and correct them later," says Mues. "It also reflects on our reputation."

At A-1 Compressor, Hepler strongly agrees. "There's no doubt about it. In the refrigeration industry mistakes can cost thousands of dollars," he says. "Preventing initial errors is the most economical way to go!"

But what effect does the existence of an extensive verification process have on initial work quality? Does its existence cause workers to be more careful or do they end up relying on the safety net of the checker?

"Workers are more precise when they know they are being checked," says Hepler. "The line employees are very much aware of expectations and we try to impress upon them that the product we put out creates our customer's perception of us. They are conscientious about doing their job right!"

Mues says a normal human reaction might be to rely on the back-up of the checking procedure, but the reputation of the designer is on the line and this encourages them to do it right the first time. At Kuether, records are kept on the projects and an entire drawing file history is retained.

"It's a learning process," says Mues. "We go back to the designer to see why a mistake was made and the process is reviewed to see if it can be prevented in the future."

The existence of quality control and accuracy verification can be an effective marketing tool for a company.

Hepler describes how customers are frequently brought in for tours to see the quality process first hand. The company's literature touts the fact that over half of their employees are involved in the quality control process. This is particularly important when dealing with a product which has much of its components enclosed in a casing. The customer must have confidence that the "guts" of that product have been put together in a quality manner.

Mues' firm talks to prospects about the quality control process utilized in their work. In some cases, especially with governmental entities, it's specifically required by the customer.

By its very nature, the word "quality" implies a company's products or services will be precise and defect-free. Any company involved in the TQM process which doesn't have this as one of its main goals is probably deluding itself and misleading its customers. The company quality leaders must devote a considerable amount of attention to setting up procedures, training, and developing a culture to encourage accuracy and attention to detail. Without this, TQM becomes little more than an exercise in cheerleading! ●••

29

Quality And
The Labor Union

Everyone is for quality, right? The answer to that qustion is more complex than it may appear.

As the quality improvement process spreads across the American business landscape some questions are being raised as to whether "quality circles," "self-directed work groups," and other forms of joint worker-management groups intrude upon the legitimate sphere of labor unions. In fact, cases before the National Labor Relations Board have intimated that, in some circumstances, they could even violate federal labor law.

The question being posed is whether or not such groups threaten workers' right to form independent unions. Overall, most worker advocacy groups welcome the increased role in decision-making and participation that TQ offers. In fact, the new competitive environment encourages workers at all levels to become business people and see the direct relation between their efforts and the prosperity and survival of their company.

"Quality is in everyone's interest," says Jim Widtfeldt of Honeywell. "It would be tragic if this worthwhile movement got derailed for some companies because of extraneous issues."

So what are the arguments being brought to bear?

In cases before the NLRB, groups such as the AFL-CIO and the Teamsters have argued that quality groups may be a form of "dummy" unions dominated by employers, especially when the purpose of such committees is to solicit worker complaints and solve employment-related problems. Some say that free choice dictates that workers should not have labor organizations forced on them.

Employer representatives have been quick to counter that the National Labor Relations Act protects employees' free choice and not necessarily unionism. Advocates of quality efforts have called for a reassessment of federal labor laws, taking into account the new realities of the workplace and the market.

A case which drew particular attention was that of Electromation, Inc.[1] where the board ruled that section 8(a)2 of the National Labor Relations Act could be used to strike down employee participation groups deemed to be "labor organizations" where their origin and existence is attributable solely to the employer and where their purpose is to deal with working condition issues and employee concerns. The NLRB held only that the activities of the employee committees at issue in the specific circumstances were a violation of the act. Three separate concurring opinions gave evidence of the considerable uncertainty that may lie ahead for some employee-participation programs, however.

The Teamsters, plaintiffs in the suit, claim that the decision sends a strong signal that employers must operate within the protections established for workers by the labor laws.

"This ruling takes the mask off employers' attempts to get around the laws that protect working people's rights to fair representation and fair treatment in the work place," says Teamster President Ron Carey. "We already have a way to establish healthy relationships between workers and management—collective bargaining. The so-called labor management 'co-operation' groups are nothing more than a management strategy to pit worker against worker and undermine workers' rights to have their voice heard through their own chosen representatives—labor unions."[2]

The applicability of this decision to all jurisdictions, and its staying power as it continues to be challenged, may well impact on the development of quality team efforts in some companies.

Despite this area of contention, many companies are developing working partnerships with organized labor as management and union begin to understand they are linked in a common partnership for survival. It is becoming more and more apparent that the interests of employers and employees are inseparable and that job security and competitiveness are essential parts of sound strategies for both business and union.

Employees seem to like involvement programs that give them the opportunity to work in partnership with management to solve problems and to bolster the overall competitiveness of the business. In fact, once brought into the process it is almost impossible to reverse worker involvement. The number of companies that have sent teams to seminars and workshops to learn principles and techniques for quality implementation is growing and, for the most part, committed management has found employees receptive and supportive of efforts to work jointly to improve quality.

Widtfeldt says that American industry is moving away from the Japanese concept of "Quality Circles" to a more comprehensive approach, stressing overall improvement of performance. With this shift occurring it would seem less likely to cause conflict with traditional labor organizations.

At my own wholesale firm in St. Louis, I found some initial uneasiness on the part of our union warehouse people as we instituted the program, but after a series of meetings and introductory exercises most people pitched in and became active participants. We proceeded by making it clear that the program was in no way intended to usurp the union's position. A separate meeting was held with the shop steward to explain the program and solicit cooperation.

Getting the support of union leadership can be difficult initially. It is important to stress that we are in a competitive contest with other companies trying to win shares of the market.

Clearly delineating working condition issues from production and service quality issues may be the key to successful continuation of programs in the face of legal challenges from organized labor. Alternatively, a recognition of the accommodation needed between labor and management would be the best solution to problems. Indeed, many companies are finding that this is possible.

Times are changing. The competitive environment we are facing is unlike any encountered before. American businesses have taken a beating in foreign trade not only because of the high cost of goods but because of a perceived lack of quality. Now, at last, we are doing something about it.

It is time to redefine the roles of management and labor to direct efforts to a common goal. Fighting "quality" and the methods used to achieve it will prove to be an exercise in futility. The businesses and unions that reject the quality approach may soon find no customers to serve and eventually no workers to employ or to organize.

It seems so obvious, but the challenges on the court dockets say otherwise.

This is where the communications skills so important to the quality process become critical. No process can succeed where a company remains divided and a segment of the company remains outside of the process. Finding a way to break down those walls and truly discover a common ground will be a key to success. ●••

30

Quality And The Bottom Line

Despite all the flag waving for Total Quality, the newspapers and trade journals in recent years still carry reports periodically about companies floundering financially even though they have undertaken extensive quality efforts.

What has gone wrong? Are these aberrations? Are there other reasons for failure or has an obsession with the paperwork and procedures inherent in formal quality processes obscured the necessary focus on the bottom line?

Don Kardux of Business Navigators says the focus on quality invariably ends up with profitability as a final result. Patience and consistency are necessary to reach this end goal, however, and where companies report poor results it may be a case where they have started the process too late. There may have been other factors leading to problems. Perhaps these companies have recovered from problems because of turning to quality.

The real issue, says Kardux, is whether the concept has been honestly embraced without just paying it lip-service. There will be inevitable resistence to management's new "quick-fix." The top and middle management must be totally committed because the front-line people will look to the top for leadership.

One of industry's chief cheerleaders for TQM is Jim Widtfeldt of Honeywell who has chaired numerous seminars on the topic.

Like Kardux, Widtfeldt says that companies embracing quality but who run into difficulty generally have other problems and quality in and of itself is not sufficient to remedy these.

"There are lots of companies who haven't bothered to investigate the quality process who are creeping to the edge of oblivion," says Widtfeldt. "People who use this as a true business improvement process are creating significant and healthy results. They may not be winning any of the quality awards but they are improving their operations."

Most people take too big of a step when they enter into a Total Quality process says Dave Gleason of Systematic Selling, Inc. The process in its infancy should be taken in small steps, like an infant learning to walk.

"What often happens," says Gleason, "is that the company focuses on things not geared to the customer and the value for which the customer is willing to pay. The quality efforts must be rewarding for customers!"

At Atlas Bolt and Screw in Ashland, Ohio, Distribution Sales and Product Manager Joseph Stager says a commitment to quality definitely contributes to a company's profitability.

"We look at rejects, reworks, lost customers. . .time is money. Do it one time and do it right and then move on to the next item," says Stager.

At Parker-Kalon, the threaded fastener division of Black and Decker, Quality Assurance Supervisor Jo Ellen Lemmon agrees that TQM bolsters profitability.

"Unfortunately," says Lemmon, "it's long-term and requires investment up front. The company must have the staying power to survive and to devote sufficient time to the process."

Lemmon feels that a company should anticipate a two to three year period before quality improvement becomes solidly locked in and all key workers and partners in the chain of product delivery understand the concepts and are indoctrinated into the need for quality. The result on the bottom line is dependent upon the time and commitment given from the top of the organization.

"If it's not there at the top the process will not be successful," says Lemmon.

In Columbus, Ohio, Leo Walsh of Columbus Temperature Control never looked at the process as a driving force toward increased profit, but rather as a management tool to ensure successful business. He feels it is important for business managers to determine what it really is that is important to them. In his mind, the way one makes a profit and the kind of service levels provided to customers is of paramount importance. Some profitable businesses never really relate to customers and their needs. Serving the marketplace is a part of quality.

At Mortemp, Inc., in Seattle, President Jerry Peterson says that when his management team first attended a quality seminar they discussed how they were going to assess the value of the program and would do it in terms of seeing how much more efficiently they would be operating. They knew they would continue to grow according to their plan, and wanted to do so without adding more "real" operating expenses.

"We are in our fourth year of TQM," says Peterson, "and we feel quality, relating both to our internal and external customers, has given us definite improvement in our operating income."

Likewise, Steve Wikstrom, vice president of manufacturing for Reell Precision Manufacturing in St. Paul, Minnesota, says concentration on quality in the right way will inevitably lead to profitability. He believes the danger in the quality process comes when a company takes a narrow focus on product only.

"Quality products are made by people with quality relationships," says Wikstrom.

Aside from being a vaccination against failure in an uncertain economy and in the midst of intense competition, can the process extricate a company from a reliance on low price as a primary marketing tool? Will it actually lead to higher gross margins?

If the customer is properly educated as to his true cost, then he may be willing to pay the higher price and support larger margins for the company providing quality levels of service and product. In a successful quality process we are looking at true partnering where "fair price" is much more important than low price.

Gleason sees the educating of the customer as being the key factor. The customers are generally willing to pay for value-added services but they must be properly selected and communicating their value is of primary importance. Generally, these features take the form of time saving for the customer, a concept which is often overlooked, but which can be readily comprehended by most customers once their attention is directed to the facts.

"In some industries people are willing to pay a higher price for quality," says Rick Mansell of Cleveland Stamping, a custom manufacturer of precision washers, nuts, and bolts. "But buyers now expect quality and to be a player in the game that is what you have to deliver."

Mansell said that it might be expected that those without a quality program might get shaken out, but this again is dependent upon the industry.

"It depends on the people you're doing business with," says Ken Urbanski, vice president of Haber Operations, manufacturer of header and nut forming tooling. "Quality translates to a tool which will last longer. If the buyer doesn't know or doesn't care then he won't be willing to pay more."

Everything may revolve around how a buyer is evaluated by his company. Is he recognized for savings up front or for long-term production savings?

"A lot of younger buyers are starting to recognize the cost of quality," says Urbanski. "They are being taught these concepts."

Wikstrom says that as a result of their emphasis on quality, "We can do things that others find difficult to do." Customers tell them that, while there are competitors knocking on their doors, they won't consider their lower prices because of the savings realized from the quality partnering relationship that exists between Reell Precision Manufacturing and their firms.

"All of our experience shows that margins can be improved," says Honeywell's Widtfeldt. "But if you can get at the excessive costs you don't need to increase margins to make more profit. Nevertheless, pleasing the customer leads to better gross margins."

The concept of shrinking costs keeps recurring when managers discuss the benefits flowing from quality improvement. An assessment of the "cost of quality" focuses on the lost time and effort as well as direct material, shipping, and labor cost involved when failed quality results in reworks, replaced product or, worse, lost customers and future profits.

"The formal process helps to identify specific costs of losses and product and service call-backs," says Widtfeldt. "When these numbers come down we know it."

Mansell pointed to the reduction in scrap achieved at his firm in Cleveland and said it had dramatically affected their bottom line. This was a readily apparent savings to Urbanski's Detroit-based company also.

"There is a cost to implement an effective program," says Stager, "but it's offset by these clearly visible savings."

The quality process itself bears a certain amount of direct costs, be it the fee of a consultant, the cost of incentives woven into the program, or the cost of manager and employee time given over to meetings, checking, or complying with additional procedures.

"We know quality costs," says Wikstrom, "but we hope it will teach us a 'smarter' way."

He cited an example from his own company where they were investigating a problem in the traditional way and had to tie up the technical people to clear up the difficulties. By empowering front-line employees, making them aware, and then shortening the cycle time, the technical people did not have to be shackled to problem solving and were free to do the job for which they were intended.

Will the impact of a quality process be seen immediately? In some small ways, the answer is yes. Employees who are invited to participate in decision-making for the first time may approach their job with a revitalized spirit. Also, the initial weeks may see an influx of suggestions and remedies for problems which should have been obvious to management.

The true impact of a program, however, can only be realized over a longer time. Typically, the first three months will be spent indoctrinating workers, setting goals, and devising an action plan. The next four to five months will be the stage for initial implementation which will involve some fine tuning and stops and starts. It may only be after this that the real, long-term impact on the bottom line may become apparent.

The length of time before pay-back becomes apparent depends on a number of factors including the size of the business, the kinds of goals set at the outset, and other programs underway and the state of the marketplace. If a company starts out with specific cost-cutting goals then perhaps these can be realized in the first six months but an actual impact on profitability will take much longer. Again, the process cannot be viewed as a band-aid and must involve permanent change in behavior and culture.

"Results can be seen immediately with the implementation of specific cost savings," says Gleason. "This will be the first positive impact of quality implementation. Things will begin to happen which will reduce costs because the company will be more modern and customer-oriented in its procedures."

It is difficult to measure one-on-one results when comparing the specific costs of setting up a program to specific cost savings. It depends on the kind of measurement established at the outset. Widtfeldt recalls a contractor he worked with who identified several key goals very succinctly set forth: (1.) Contract retention by per cent; (2.) Growing new contracts by per cent; (3.) Reducing call-backs related to condenser failure by seventy-five per cent; and (4.) Reducing call-backs due to air flow problems.

The very specific nature of these initial goals allowed measurement and a clear picture of immediate savings. Where initial goals are broader in scope it may take longer to realize actual savings. Nevertheless, the broader the scope of desired change the greater the potential to really make a difference in the business' operation. Kardux observes that businesses setting out on a quality improvement process will tend to show a one to two per cent increase in the bottom line during the first year.

Noting that number one in the hierarchy of needs of the individual worker is a feeling that he or she is making a contribution to his organization, Kardux says that when management and employees begin to work as a team the worker is more satisfied and inevitably becomes more productive. The end result is a group of people (the workers) who in a certain sense "own" the company.

In summary, quality does not in itself guarantee profitability or even survival. It is one of many factors that determines who will win the competitive race. Focusing on quality will, however, ensure that a company will be a robust player in the game. ●●•

31

Benchmarking In The Quality Process

How do you stack up to the other guy?

In a sophisticated way, that's the question quality professionals ask when they take part in the process referred to as "benchmarking."

More than just a buzz word, this is a means of finding out how you are doing in relation to the best performers inside and out of your industry. It refers to comparing what you're doing in a very open way and opening up all but the most proprietary information to other companies. By so doing a company is able to see how effectively it is performing in the marketplace versus its competition or other industrial companies. Once a good evaluation is made it then becomes easier to set attainable goals.

Benchmarking can be a device to get management to "buy in" to the quality philosophy. In checking out other companies which are successfully carrying out TQ, management can see the positive impact of the process and can see that lofty goals can indeed be achieved. It therefore can be an effective way to garner strong top management commitment where the original impetus has come not from the top but from a quality-oriented middle manager.

As the United States begins to compete in a world-wide economy, benchmarking becomes more important than ever. We find ourselves competing not just against each other but against totally different labor forces and business mind-sets and against countries with different work cultures. World-wide, expectations develop for product and service quality and it is important for the company competing in that arena to have a good understanding of what those expectations will be.

Benchmarking can be a formal process or very informal, oftentimes depending on the size of a company and the strength of its manufacturing orientation. Most agree, however, that some kind of criteria need to be established.

It's more than two companies merely talking together. If we get too rigid we won't have a free exchange of information. It needs to be determined in advance what direction and path the company will follow.

At Reell Manufacturing in St. Paul, Steve Wikstrom says the company approaches benchmarking from an informal standpoint.

"We take advantage of and provide opportunities for people to see us and for us to see them. We call it networking. We invite people in the twin cities to come in and view our operations and give us their observations of what they see."

Wikstrom describes the company's "non-customer tour days," held on the first Tuesday of each month. On these days the company is opened up to the community. Representatives of other companies come in to learn how Reell has applied the quality process. Tour groups are taken through each functional area and workers in that group rotate serving as spokesperson for the group. The day ends with a box lunch where managers and workers sit down and talk with visitors about what they have seen and exchange ideas for improvement.

The idea for this came from Baldrige Award winner Zytec Corporation, also headquartered in Minnesota, who used this "open-house" concept in a more formalized way. Due to the relatively small size of Reell, this exchange of information works better than a structured benchmarking process.

"A lot of benefits flow from these subtle forms of cooperation that help companies do things more effectively and efficiently," says Wikstrom. "This is especially so if you exchange cross-functional groups with other companies."

Reell Manufacturing has been active in the local chamber of commerce and participates in joint training with other companies. This organization also gives managers a platform to evangelize for their TQM philosophies. Reell sends several people to regular meetings of the "North Central Deming Forum," a group of companies following quality guru W. Edwards Deming's theories.

The larger the company the more likely that the benchmarking process will be formally established. At Southwestern Bell Telephone, the

TQM: *Reports From The Front Lines*

division of Southwestern Bell Corporation, Area Quality Manager Mike Berry says they follow a systematic approach in that they use a consulting firm to direct the process. This is normally a Big Six accounting firm that specializes in gathering information and putting consortiums of companies together for exchanges of information.

"I'm somewhat skeptical of the methodology used in large scale studies," says Berry. "They study a small part of Southwestern Bell, not the whole, and this may not be representative."

Berry stresses the importance of keeping the benchmarking process under control in large companies or there is a risk of being buried in data. He breaks the process down into two areas—functional and competitive.

"In the functional area we benchmark our own internal processes against the potential capabilities if we were to acquire the proper technology," says Berry. "In competitive benchmarking we go out and see what our direct competitors are doing to help guide our efforts. We actually refer to it not as benchmarking but 'competitive analysis.'"

Berry cautions that the benefits of benchmarking can only flow as long as it is done right. If not done well a company can harm itself because they will not be comparing against the right competitors or similar companies. There is a risk that the company can be lulled into a false sense of security. Besides, it's not always what the competition is doing today but what they will be doing tomorrow. Benchmarking looks at what is happening now, and does not look into the future. The biggest threat may come from competitors who don't even exist at the time. Berry cites the telephone industry as an example. Benchmarking may compare against other telecommunication companies, but a few years into the future the company may be competing against cable TV companies or some other entities.

What criteria is used to select what items are to be benchmarked?

Bill Beck of Precisionaire in St. Petersburg, Florida, says a decison must be made as to what area is the most significant. This involves taking a look at production, customer service, accounting, distribution and other areas. The companies against which comparisons should be made are selected for different reasons. Perhaps they are active in the Baldrige process. Maybe they have a strong market share or are noted for having good systems in place. Companies can also be selected by reading material in trade journals about innovative companies, or checking out some of the "one-hundred best companies" type of publications that are continually being published.

Before a lot of time is invested in benchmarking it is important to know where a company is going in the quality effort. Have specific problem areas arisen which call for attention? The path of inquiry must be determined and the TQ effort must be in place.

Every area of the company can be benchmarked in some form or another. The various systems and departments can be studied but you will want to isolate specific problems to be sure not to overload that task with benchmarking targets. For all the specific areas you want to look into, you must have your TQ effort in place with success already established in the basics.

Like the basketball player who uses a piece of chalk to mark the highest point of his jump and then continually tries to better that jump, the benchmarking process allows companies to select realistic, yet proven and attainable goals. What better measurement than to find out how you stack up against the competition?

Benchmarking, both formal and informal, will help you to assess where you stand! ●••

32

Quality And The Computer

As the quality revolution unfolded in America and around the world, the computer revolution also was charging full speed ahead. Throughout industry personal computers were showing up on people's desks. Data processing was not just the province of a separate DP department. The proliferation of software programs and management's comfort level with computerized reports and information dovetailed neatly into quality-based systems such as statistical process control, just-in-time delivery, and monitoring of service levels.

"I don't think you can manage what you can't measure!" says Marge Yonda of Computer Solutions of Rochester, New York. "With the right software tools you can evaluate performance and processes. Otherwise, you'll spend a lot of time and money and may find yourself dead in the water."

Yonda is an independent computer consultant who assists companies in the selection, design, and implementation of their data-processing systems. Her writings on DP related topics appear extensively in numerous trade magazines.

Scott Stratman of software vendor R & D Systems, in Colorado Springs, agrees that the DP system is a tool to be used not only to collect data, but to measure effectiveness of operations. Depending on the system, a company now has the capability to track and report the most minute details of a process. The ability to "roll up" those details into concise summaries for management allows a constant review of service levels. A good DP environment enables an organization to slice and dice the information many different ways, depending upon needs and whatever problems they are trying to correct.

But doesn't the TQM process focus on people? Does the involvement of the computer detract from this orientation?

"Not necessarily," says Yonda. "You have to uncover where quality improvement is necessary and evaluate what went wrong. It's then up to management to come up with projects for people to solve the problem."

Yonda cites the example of a company which is trying to determine why they are seeing an increase in credit memorandums. The only way to investigate this on a large scale is to code the credit memos and assess why they are happening. It is time-consuming to do this manually but, with a computer, "reason codes" can be asssigned at the time of credit memo preparation and then statistical summaries of reasons for occurrence can be readily available. In this way the system can save time for people, who then focus on evaluation and planning.

Stratman says the role of data processing in the quality process is to provide ammunition to teams and quality leaders so they can be more proactive in preventing and resolving problems.

"If you have an understanding of what it is your customers look to you for, having confidence in your data allows your customer service people to better meet those needs," says Stratman.

Mike Orso of General Data Systems in St. Louis says the DP system in any company impacts on customer service and the way employees relate to external customers.

"The computer systems should play a key role in meeting customer expectations," says Orso. "Your customer contact people will be able to give accurate answers and information will flow to customers at a much faster pace."

It is not uncommon for people to make joking references to the computer department's inability to speak the same language as other employees and customers. This can be a problem in the quality process.

Stratman sees the separate data-processing department as a thing of the past. It is now integrated with other facets of small business operation and almost everyone in the organization will be "on line" frequently.

Yonda agrees that in small companies a separate DP department seldom exists. Key line managers or the principals of the company are generally involved. Large companies are still likely to have separate departments.

"Where you still have separate departments, you'll have departmental conflict," says Orso. "A DP system on its own won't solve conflicts but can help overcome these problems."

Orso gives an example of a client where there was a continuing conflict between accounting and inside sales. The accounting department objected to the way that inside sales was filling out order forms for transfer to accounting where they were entered into the computer. With today's technology the order is entered at the same time, so there is no split function between customer service and data processing. Of course, the accounting department might object to being taken out of the sequence, but the net effect is for the walls to come down within a company and procedures to be compressed into fewer steps.

In many companies the data-base administrator plays a key role in developing the Total Quality process.

"In any consulting I've done," says Stratman, "if the DP manager is not on the steering committee then that committee gets its information second hand. The role of the DP administrator on the committee will depend on his or her personality and communication skills as well as the structure of the company."

As Total Quality becomes more of a focus throughout industry, so too does it become the subject of specialized software development. Yonda, Stratman, and Orso report that the kind of measurements utilized in TQ tend to be integrated into the new standard packages rather than being separately labeled as TQ programs. Specialized training in Total Quality applications of data-processing is beginning to be offered.

"The software system has to be able to accumulate errors on its own," says Yonda. "A computer can capture such things as late orders and help a company see if the problem is caused by a vendor or its own people."

She says the computer should have a "stop" feature that would allow information about a non-quality event to be entered.

What about DP vendors and consultants themselves? Are they being called upon to serve as partners in the quality process of their clients?

"If I don't provide Total Quality service I don't have a client!" says Yonda.

Stratman is seeing this in a variety of forms. Some customers actually send teams to do audits of his service. Orso reports certain of the larger companies working with General Data are monitoring quality standards of performance under specific programs.

This is a slowly growing phenomenon.

"When we get calls for help our customers expect us to know what to do," says Orso. "We have to be on top of the technology so we can be not only reactive but proactive."

System users, too, report that fully utilizing a modern DP system enhances their quality effort.

"We use our system to help in evaluating our vendors," says President Stan Hurt of Indiana Supply. "We track such things as back orders, errors in shipment, and other measures. If a vendor's evaluation indicates a problem we will call them in for a meeting to correct the situation. Errors are also tracked by customer to help us evaluate the profitability of given customers."

"This is where the program starts to pay off," says Hurt. "Until you can evaluate what is happening you don't know whether or not you are improving!"

At Airguard Industries, Inc., in Louisville, Quality Control Manager Jeff Holmes says their software package is used to evaluate vendors of raw materials based on key criteria such as product weight or critical dimensions. For each vendor they establish a process average and can have hard data with which to approach vendors if performance is slipping. At the same time, there is growing pressure from the company's large OEM customers and government contractors to meet structured quality standards and participate in vendor rating systems.

Stratman compares the relation of Total Quality Management and data-processing to the current state of electronic data interchange and bar coding. These are topics which are receiving a lot of attention in many industries without full utilization of all the capabilities available. He sees Total Quality on about the same place on the continuum of customer acceptance.

The computer alone is not the answer to the needs of Total Quality, but it can make the process quicker and more precise.

"Once the problem is defined you can then select an area where you can shoot for something better," says Yonda. "You have to put the people in place to make it happen."

Like many facets of Total Quality, data-processing provides the tools. It is up to management to provide the training and motivation for people to use those tools. ●●•

33

*Quality And
Asset Protection*

For some reason management, in its drive toward TQM, has continually failed to protect the assets it has amassed. For unexplained reasons, be it ignorance or a lack of direction, management has abdicated responsiblity in the area of asset protection. Companies have looked the other way or used approaches guided by anecdotal rather than real information, says Terrence J. Korpal, retired United States Secret Service agent and a leading consultant on corporate asset protection.

Korpal, with twenty-five years of experience in federal and local law enforcement and currently a member of the graduate faculty of Webster University, is founder and president of Korpal Associates. The firm provides investigation, training, consulting, and electronic counter measures to major companies and law firms throughout the midwest.

At first glance it would seem an emphasis on asset protection and corporate security is inconsistent with TQM. Does not the quality process promote openness and sharing of techniques and information? Does it not empower employees to take "ownership" of their company?

Korpal says this inconsistency is a misperception. Quality management creates a sense of ownership and belonging, however it must be truly adhered to instead of just given lip service. If employees are given shared access they then should be held responsible and accountable if assets are lost as a result.

"Involving employees in asset protection rekindles in them a certain belief in the company largesse and responsiveness to needs," says Korpal. "The majority of employees are honest and decent. When exceptions are made and the parameter of acceptable conduct is widened, it allows erosion of values and weakened adherence to company policy."

Part of this process is the implementation of management's desired goals as restated through their policies. If the CEO has an idea, it may get watered down and supervisors interpret this in the light of what they feel is fair. Failure by managers and staff to allocate accountability decreases this adherence and creates an opportunity for theft and other misconduct. The remedy, says Korpal, is totally open communication which explains how the company works and how a lack of theft benefits the entire corporate community. This open communication creates a better asset protection program than anyone could hope to fashion unilaterally.

Is limiting information to only specified people inconsistent with theories underlying Total Quality? If we are talking about information such as trade secrets and company strategies it is foolish to allow everyone to share in that information prior to publication or prior to its implementation because, like it or not, it is a fact of corporate life that not all employees are totally committed to the company goals. Further, there has been an increase in corporate espionage because competitors find it far less expensive to obtain information this way than to create their own marketing and sales plan. Not every employee has a hand in selling goods and therefore not everyone needs all the information that might harm the company or impede its sales. This does not negate total quality.

Korpal observes that many firms relegate security to a maintenance man, groundskeeper, or a low-paid watchman—the very people who, away from normal business hours, have access to and control of almost all assets of importance to the company. With internal theft outstripping external by a ratio of four to one, he stresses that modern asset protection management should be given the same attention as legal, accounting, and marketing concerns.

Active theft prevention programs send a message to the work force that management is seriously interested in regaining or maintaining control of its destiny and that it will set, implement, and execute policies designed to make the company as profitable as possible. When a company suffers internal theft and no steps are taken to address the problem, employees may begin to ignore management suggestions and directives in other areas. Time and again studies have demonstrated that workers are happier when there are active internal theft counter measures in place.

When the company ignores theft, it reduces the ability of honest employees to fight off efforts of the dishonest workers to steal outright or to justify what they are taking as wages in kind.

Korpal tells stories of honest employees coming forward to provide information to investigators shortly after prevention programs have begun. They often state that they are relieved that management is showing determination to bring permissiveness to an end and stop neglect that has allowed theft to continue unabated. The overall effect on esprit de corps is positive where efforts are made to stop theft which has been previously tolerated.

Does a prevention program imply that management doesn't trust employees? Not at all! It merely puts workers on notice that management is going to manage the business.

Dishonesty in the workplace has been on the rise in recent years, notes Korpal. This may be a result of the loss of social mores, the increased complexity of data-processing systems and managements' failure to comprehend those systems, and may be aggravated by recessionary economic conditions. Theft goes beyond cash or pecuniary assets, however, and may involve the taking of confidential data, marketing strategies, customer lists, or other confidential information.

Another area often forgotten is "time theft" which may not even be perceived by employees as defrauding their company. This issue of time theft plays a factor as the United States competes in the international marketplace. According to Korpal the Japanese have very little internal theft while the American worker steals annually 240 hours on the average. This translates to a tremendous amount of money and puts the U.S. at a significant disadvantage in the marketplace.[1]

There are as many fraud schemes in the market as there are days in the year and hours in the day. These range from defrauding the company by use of telephones, credit cards, watts lines, personal use of office machinery, kick-backs, theft of merchandise, to collusion with vendors. The computer has created many more opportunities for fraud. The extent of the problem can depend on how management handles computer accessibility.

More opportunity for theft exists today because both management and workers ignore available computer security procedures. Computers allow companies to set up base parameters in a recording system to identify things occurring outside those parameters. Nevertheless, companies seldom go beyond cursory comments about responsibility for passwords into the system. How can a company protect itself? Korpal states that management should use the same kind of judgement it uses for establishing marketing plans, designing computer programs, or other critical functions. A professional should be consulted or added to staff to provide modern professional procedures and policies.

A professional asset protection manager should have adequate training in procedures and policies to prevent asset loss. Companies can install professional alarm systems in addition to a human physical presence capable of meeting court challenges to security enforcement.

Korpal counsels companies to begin protection efforts by preventing access to confidential or valuable items. This begins at the entrance to the grounds. Companies should evaluate the crime in their neighborhood and determine how to stop it from happening on their own property or parking lot. The easiest way is generally through modern access and control systems which are computerized and which allow access by special cards. The same systems can also track time and attendance.

Modern access systems can have as many as 150 different zones. The CEO could access all zones but part-time clerks might have limited access to specified areas at specified times and days—or at flexible, varied times. All of this activity is recorded and, through software, can be reported.

Additional access control devices include monitored cameras. Where the size of a company allows, a security person should be devoted to monitoring the screens. This is not an easy task and requires concentration. Korpal says that most businesses have designed their security programs to prevent the public from walking away with assets, but the biggest threat generally comes from within. Keeping this internal threat in mind, it is important that detailed attention be given to the hiring process. A thorough screening is the single most effective and cost efficient tool. A thorough background check should be carried out with possible use of psychological testing to help the human resources department.

A preventive program can also turn attention to procedures for shipping, receiving, how confidential data is moved from one location to another and where it is stored, how material of a confidential nature will be disposed of, and what situations might arise that will increase risk.

It is poor management to wait until a disaster strikes to deal with security problems. If labor unrest exists, if the area is subject to weather disasters, or if products or equipment pose the potential for disaster, then security planning should be done in advance so that all systems are ready when needed.

Emphasizing again the importance of devoting quality management time to asset protection, Korpal reports that he generally sees management of security delegated to someone as a secondary task. Security or safety executives often have no experience in this area which leaves the company open to lawsuit or loss.

"Corporate managers are generally as ill-equipped to make asset protection decisions as they are to conduct bone surgery," says Korpal.

How does security affect customer service levels? Good asset protection should prevent the loss of product, poor inventory control, the loss of orders, and increases in operational costs. Losses may actually go beyond the cost of the disappearing material. Where inventory is missing, failure to ship that material may result in the loss of future business due to the loss of goodwill resulting from the broken promise. Items often have a higher replacement cost as prices of replacement inventory rise. To this must be added the cost of repackaging, insurance, shipping costs, additional labor, and the drain on management working on problem resolution. Due to the time and preoccupation which often results, internal theft reduces the ability of executives to deal effectively with customers.

It is important to prosecute transgressors who are apprehended. Too often companies listen to their attorneys and don't prosecute in order to avoid lawsuits. Attorneys are running the businesses and business managers are running scared.

"Arrest and prosecution of internal thieves is the single most effective tool. Find them. Fire them. Arrest them. That is best for the company," says Korpal.

As the competitiveness of the marketplace increases, so does corporate espionage and the gathering of corporate intelligence. This means it is incumbent on all companies to consider protection of trade secrets and marketing strategy.

Corporate espionage is the illegal gathering of information whereas corporate intelligence is the legal gathering of information. Intelligence is a rapidly growing area in which people trained in this discipline are employed by a variety of firms to research and analyze competitor's information available by legal means. Foreign countries are using their intelligence agencies to get this type of information, viewing corporate intelligence as another aspect of national defense. They don't hesitate to use all manner of methods against firms doing business in their countries, competing with their native firms, and putting employees out of work.

Korpal stresses again the strategy of reducing access and the use of electronic countermeasures wherever information is transmitted (i.e., fax, computer lines, telephones, etc.).

Does the idea of limiting access to certain areas (tool rooms or certain inventory items, for example), impede the high levels of customer service sought in a quality process? Not at all! Management must devise methods, manage those methods, and hold people accountable to serve the customers totally. Limiting access, after effective pre-employment screening, is the single most effective asset protection measure available to management. As the Total Quality program progresses, procedures which allow incremental access to more areas may be effective, however, this is doomed to failure if there is slippage in dedication to TQM which holds managers and employees accountable.

What about the impact on employee feelings of "ownership" of their companies if access is restricted? The real answer is that this depends on how well managers communicate. Many employees are comforted by bounds and boundaries. This is a normal feeling in all areas of life, and social order translates in the business environment to corporate order. The thinking is "I'm not supposed to be in this area and do not have responsibility for what transpires in this area. Therefore I'm neither responsible nor accountable." The employee need not share in the blame or awkward feelings if members of the corporation are suspected of theft.

One factor to be considered in instituting a more stringent security program is the involvement of labor unions in a given business. The reaction of unions often varies. Companies do make a major mistake when they implement security policies or renew old policies without explanations to the work force of the need for these policies. The goals must be clearly stated along with the reasons why such policies are needed. Professional asset protection management should include communication to all levels of employees to point out how everyone derives benefits from the new policies.

A factor which also must be considered is the increase in substance abuse. The workplace is a microcosm of society at large and suffers the same problems. This abuse results in increased sick days, loss of productivity, theft of assets, and more accidents.

This creates a potentially expensive litigation problem for most companies where employees and the public are in danger when people under the influence of illegal substances are operating equipment. It is far more cost-effective, says Korpal, to prevent occurrences and avoid bringing this problem into the workplace than to support the treatment of those in the workforce suffering from abuse. Workers should be educated as to the effects of substance abuse, and management personnel can be trained to recognize such problems in their areas.

Supervisors and managers must face up to their problems with courage. Too often managers working away from the eyes of higher level executives are intimidated by employees to the point where they overlook theft. Employees and managers are often afraid to call a crime a crime, says Korpal. To help in this area, top management needs ready access and frequent contact with the work areas. Shipping and receiving should be physically separated and employee parking lots ideally are located some distance from loading docks. The idea is to design a plant layout so that it is difficult for an employee to take material from the dock to a personal vehicle without being noticed.

Asset protection management, according to Korpal, focuses on what is known as the "Four A's." These are:

- *Awareness—Businesses should consider employee education, seminars, meetings, and training.*

- *Audit—Methods must be researched, tested, put in writing, enforced, and constantly reviewed.*

- *Apprehension—Utilize both civil and criminal penalties against both internal and external theft without exception.*

- *Area—Define which areas of personnel are experiencing the most problems with inventory shrinkage, productivity, high workmen's compensation claims, refunded sales, and cash shortages.*

Employees, not employers, determine the boundaries of production theft and deviation from acceptable work practices.

"All employees don't steal," says Korpal, "but if theft and internal misconduct is left unchecked, uncontrolled, or unchallenged, then the effectiveness of management is undermined, and morale is damaged. Management effectively forfeits control and authority and replaces it with informal standards set by employees and low-level supervisors."

Unfortunately, it is too easy for employees to think that if management doesn't care then there is no need for them to be concerned.

While employee theft and misconduct continues to reduce profits, losses can be reduced by effective programs. This includes proactive preemployment policies and the creation of a working environment in which theft is unacceptable.

Quality management can take a number of steps to ensure protection of assets:

1. *Management must take the business as a whole and survey the corporation for vulnerability, looking at the potential for human and asset loss either by theft or violence.*

2. *Having surveyed, the data must be evaluated and analyzed.*

3. *Examine alternatives across the board, including professional asset protection measures.*

4. *Implement the desired measures after choosing the method most applicable to the corporate culture.*

5. *Set up procedures for consistent and continuous review of the systems and parameters that have been established.*

6. *Modify or adjust these systems as they develop, consistent with the quality management program.*

An effective asset protection program can restore management control. Every business can ensure its maximum profitability and the welfare of its shareholders with a minimum expenditure. ●●•

34

The War On Drugs And A Quality Work Environment

"**M**r. Johnson, I have a very serious problem I need to talk to you about."

The owner, manager, or supervisor of a business of any appreciable size has probably had the experience of being approached by an employee who confides that he or she has a chemical abuse problem. This usually comes about because some other event or person in the employee's life has brought the problem to a head and forced the employee to confront the problem and seek treatment.

The flip side of this is where a problem remains hidden and the company is sitting on a time bomb. Somewhere within the organization is a person who may be driving vehicles, handling cash, climbing on ladders, or dealing with complex technical assignments while under the influence of mind-altering chemicals.

In today's society this is a reality and it is something that the company instituting a Total Quality Process must deal with if the open communication, trust, and empowerment of TQ is to be effective.

"Misuse of drugs and alcohol injures relationships between workers and supervisors which are essential for the successful implementation of TQ processes," says Patrick Openlander, a psychologist who advises businesses regarding impaired employees. "Further, excessive ingestion of alcohol and drugs or the misuse of prescription medications has a scientifically documented negative effect on coordination and judgement, thus affecting equipment use."

Openlander, who received specialized training at the Duke University Alcohol Institute under the auspices of Anheuser-Busch Employee Assistance Programs, says the misuse of drugs or alcohol by a worker promotes many attitudes and behaviors detrimental to cooperation.

"Secrecy, lethargy, irritability, and confusion are common results of drug abuse," says Openlander. "All of these patterns reduce the bonds of trust and the sense of common purpose needed in a TQ program. In addition, they create unpredictability which also lowers trust."

Impaired workers are in no position to participate successfully in a movement requiring clarity of thinking, responsibility, and honesty, says Openlander. Just as damaging, co-workers may act out of a sense of divided loyalties to draw attention away from the substance abuser, cover up mistakes, or otherwise prevent a productive allocation of responsibilities. Substance abusers often attempt to create a subculture of secrecy and permissiveness which competes directly with the goals of a TQ program. All of these factors, according to Openlander, act to undermine the values of a TQ process.

A worker who one day is focused and productive, and the next day withdrawn and slow, makes follow through on decisions and consistency almost impossible.

The problem is out there and cannot be ignored. On its face it seems so alien to the basic mission of running a profitable business, yet in today's culture it is a problem which is often dumped in the lap of the business owner who finds himself acting "in loco parentis" to help the employee come to grips with it, or to protect other employees from hazards created by the abuser.

This task is either made easier or more difficult (depending on one's perspective) by the provisions of the federal Drug Free Workplace Act. The Act, which applies to those with federal government contracts in excess of $25,000, requires that a drug-free awareness program must be established to inform employees of the dangers of drug abuse, and calls for establishing drug-free policies, counseling and employee assistance programs, and clarifying penalties to be assessed for drug abuse violations.[1]

To those who would say that drug usage is a private matter and not the concern of the employer, one could point to a study of the effects of drug use on work habits published in the November 1990 *Journal of the American Medical Association.* The study, conducted by the medical school of the University of Iowa, followed the work habits of some 2500 Boston postal workers, some of whom had tested positive for drugs in pre-employment testing. In five major areas of work behavior (absenteeism, turn-over, accidents, injuries, and discipline infractions) the marijuana and co-caine users were found to exhibit these problems with a frequency rate consistently higher than that of non-users. While this study used ad-vanced statistical models to accurately reflect the difference between users and non-users, previous studies have shown even poorer performance for drug users.[2]

It seems clear from these studies, and is just common sense, that not only are drug users less efficient employees, but they pose a real threat to the health and safety of their co-workers and therefore also put the com-pany at risk from a liability standpoint.

Will employees accept a drug and alcohol policy? If a company oper-ates delivery services, employs truck drivers, or comes within the provi-sions of the Act described above then they will have little choice. A policy must be implemented and the law's requirements will supersede any union contract provisions or employee preferences. What impact does the implementation of such a program have on the company's TQ process?

Openlander says the emphasis on closer coordination and communi-cation makes these two efforts synergistic.

"TQM places more responsibility with workers and creates greater pressure to communicate effectively," he says. "This helps surface sub-stance abuse problems more quickly, thus making the availability of ser-vices to assist the abuser even more vital."

Good substance abuse programming is designed to produce honesty and directness in communication, so it fits neatly into the drive for coop-eration and efficiency in TQM. But merely stating and enforcing a pro-gram places the entire burden on the employer. How can we foster a cor-porate culture that refuses to sanction chemical abuse and helps root out the problem in a firm but compassionate way?

Employees will respond positively to programs that do not encourage favoritism or special treatment, that place an emphasis on prevention, but show a willingness to work with first-time offenders in resolving their problems. They will expect consequences to be clearly defined and em-ployee privacy and dignity to be respected.

Despite the perception that drugs are widespread in the workplace, many see this as a great social evil and readily support measures to bring it under control, even at the expense of some loss of privacy. On the other hand, few wish to come forward and identify the abusers within their midst. There seems to be a feeling that it's "the company's problem" and they wait for management to act, all the while wondering, "Why don't they do something about it?"

This attitude of not getting involved does place the burden on supervisors to be alert for telltale signs or problems indicating chemical abuse which affect job performance or which could create safety problems. An established drug policy which calls for drug testing when there is reasonable cause to believe a problem exists affecting work performance can be the framework within which action can be taken.

Gaining employee support for a program will be easiest where it is made clear that workers who voluntarily come forward to deal with their problems will be given support and time to deal with their problems, at least within the guidelines of existing leave and vacation policies. This does not mean that they should be exempt from the consequences of their actions as they impact upon the company's work or products. Violations of work rules which result from chemical abuse (i.e., theft, absence, safety violations, etc.) should be dealt with without looking to the chemical problem as a mitigating circumstance. The company performance standards cannot be lowered or allowed to deteriorate merely because of a problem of this nature. A profit-making enterprise must continue to fulfill its prime mission even while it attempts to play a role in resolving societal problems.

What about the recovering substance-abuser's participation in the quality process? Can he or she be an effective contributor?

Openlander says that at the heart of most substance abuse treatment is the famous "twelve steps" approach. These tenets emphasize intense self-scrutiny and a deep commitment to constant renewal and service. Consequently, a successfully treated substance abuser can make an excellent team member. He or she has already made a promise to be open to new information and admit mistakes.

"The question of suitability for leadership of teams or exercises within the quality process is a more complex issue," says Openlander. "In the immediate aftermath of treatment, there may be a period of instability that shows up in shame or a compensatory euphoria in the treated person, and co-workers may be uncertain of the ability of the successfully treated person."

Openlander suggests that it may be helpful to wait for a period of months for the treatment and aftercare processes to mature before advancing a former substance abuser to a leadership role. The recently treated person can and should be asked "how their program is going" and whether they are keeping up with aftercare. Mainly, he says, the person recently completing treatment should be allowed to readjust slowly and, if their behavior is stable for a period of months, they should be asked confidentially if they feel ready to take on leadership responsibilities.

The company concerned with providing quality service and products will respond to a chemical abuse situation in an even-handed way.

Management knows its success depends upon quality people. Proper selection, vigilent supervisors, and a firm and well-planned program for salvaging those who still have the potential to contribute will send the right message and help bring all workers into the effort. ●●•

35

Quality And
The Competition

Much has been said and written about quality in terms of being the best a company can be, continually improving, and meeting customer expectations. But what does this mean in the context of a competitive struggle in a finite market? Is TQM competition oriented or is it a win-win proposition for the country and industry over-all?

"Somebody is going to lose," says consultant Dave Gleason. "We can't say we'll all be winners! The concept of quality as value-added selling fits in well no matter how hard a sell you must use."

Stan Hurt of Indiana Supply says that all of the ingredients of intense competition still remain. Price will always be there, he says, no matter what people may say—and the better the company has adapted to the quality process, the more costs will drop, and the more price competitive the company will be.

"As your costs drop it gives you the ability to compete down and dirty," says Hurt.

Don Kardux of Business Navigators sees the impact of Total Quality from a different perspective.

"It is definitely not competition oriented," says Kardux. "In industry today we are often confused about who are our competitors. As we raise the level of quality for our industry the result is increased business for everyone!"

"I cringe at the philosophy of 'guerrilla marketing' and other battle terms," says Kardux. "Quality is the most powerful force to bring the consumer to you since the consumer is driven by his own self-interest, and if you are providing more quality in your products or service you can't lose. This is a positive rather than a negative approach to marketing."

Gleason argues that the foundation of all success is relationship selling—getting your customers totally involved in the partnership process and inter-relating with the customer's needs and desires. It's all a matter of finding a niche and putting yourself there.

"Quality is a value-added service which makes a customer feel that he's working with a company responsive to his needs," says Gleason. "The whole process is a two-way street."

Can Total Quality be viewed and used as a competitive weapon? Hurt responds affirmatively. "It's definitely one of our sales tools," he says. "We stress the fact that we will serve our customers correctly the first time."

"Quality is something salespeople should have been focusing on all along," says Gleason. "It is the essence of a sale."

If everybody in the world uses the word "quality" it becomes meaningless. The real question is how quality is manifested? All of the different things we do add up to quality service and it's these individual things that need to be communicated to the customer.

"You need to think 'What am I proud of?'" says Kardux. "For example, I remember a heating contractor in Erie, Pennsylvania, who has the homeowner climb up a ladder and look down the trunk line of ductwork. The contractor puts a light in the duct and seriously asks 'Isn't that beautiful?'"

It is just this type of sincere communicating of the special values added which effectively convey a company's quality message. People know that they get only what they pay for and, if we try to sell them on the idea of quality service without specifics, they will be saying in the back of their mind, "What is it I'm not getting?"

Do customers view specific talk about TQ as irrelevant hocus-pocus? Are we best to just shut up and deliver or should we be talking about it specifically?

Gleason cautions that, unless the customer is somehow involved in the process itself, talk should center exclusively on the value-added results of quality. However, if the customer is a business involved in the process itself, then it is helpful and appropriate to talk the jargon of TQ. This may be especially true if the customer is a large enterprise, with a formal quality control department, who is looking to your company to fit within their system. For example, at Brauer Supply in St. Louis our customer base is divided into small contractors and large industrial businesses. We have found that quality must be communicated in a quite different fashion to these two kinds of buyers.

When the competitor is pushing his own quality attributes how should we respond?

"My counsel is to ignore them," says Kardux. "We spend too much time focusing on our competitition and not on what we are doing and can do for our customer! I liken dealing with your competitors to dealing with a group of two-year olds. If they're squalling just ignore them and after a while they'll go away."

"Never downgrade or complain about anyone else," says Hurt. "If we all do a good job it will still come down to salesmanship."

While we are still in a competitive environment, what is the effect of trade associations and chambers of commerce, etc., promoting TQM as a win-win proposition for everyone?

Kardux is a strong proponent of sharing quality concepts with other businesses. "I often suggest calling the competition to see what works for them," he says. "Again, I stress the concept that a rising tide will raise all ships."

Gleason is more restrictive from this standpoint, arguing that you get to a certain point in working with competitors where problems can develop.

"Information shared with you by customers should be used to your best advantage," says Gleason. "If you do the sharing in a group or an association it should be on a very general level, not specific. People in the same industry can gain a lot from interchange if they are in different geographical markets and are not competitors."

When you are not going head-to-head with a company, sharing specific experiences and means of resolving problems can be helpful.

Utilizing Total Quality in the sales pitch to customers creates a danger of overpromising and failing. Credibility can suffer as well as the business manager's own sense of internal honesty. If we know we are unable to ship by Tuesday, but nevertheless promise to meet that deadline to get an order, it not only affects our credibility with the customer but it does insidious damage to our own staff internally. They begin to question the integrity of the company's customer service commitment.

"If you make a promise, you had better deliver," says Hurt. "The competition will pick up on your failure. Beware!"

There can be a tendency for people afraid of the rough and tumble competition of the business world to seize upon TQM as a sort of "nice-guy" namby-pamby program that will provide a ready excuse to avoid head-to-head combat.

"If we mean rough and tumble competition as ruthless, under-handed saber-slashing then yes—it can avoid this," says Kardux, "But that isn't the way to go to market. The American consumer is now educated. Free lunches and special deals are out. The customer knows he's paying for it."

Kardux says we need to get away from the "I killed 'em" style of selling and begin to see the salesperson as a counselor.

Gleason says, however, that quality should not numb one's competitive instinct. He says that, to a certain extent, we are engaged in a war and quality must indeed be a weapon in that war.

"Total Quality can bring about a win-win situation," he says, "but not for you and your competitor. The winners must be you and your customer in the mutually advantageous partnership you create!" ●●•

36

*Quality And
Inventory Management*

Quality touches every part of a business and almost every enterprise is dependent upon effective management of inventory in some form or another. The ability for a manufacturer to have raw materials in place and on hand at the proper time or the success of a sales and distribution company in securing product in a timely fashion and having it on the shelf when its customers need it will impact on the service levels provided and the extent to which customer requirements will be met.

In today's fast-paced environment business customers, especially manufacturing firms, have begun to demand "Just In Time" delivery from their suppliers. Theoretically, they expect material for their needs to arrive in a narrow window of time just before they will call for that material's use. This requires working with a vendor to ensure that sufficient inventory is on-hand in the vendor's warehouse or, carried to its fullest extent, material is stationed in a public warehouse or other repository near the point of use where the customer can draw upon that material when needed.

"JIT is a part of quality service which organizations must provide if their customers demand it," says Keith Dierberg of Concordia University. "The customer is constantly redefining quality and if he defines quality as having the product there on Thursday for work in process on Friday we may not be able to ship days or weeks in advance."

This can create stress and bottlenecks in the shipping process and the quality supplier will develop systems to monitor and expedite shipments to keep this to a minimum. The goal is for the customer's hassles to be reduced so that it is easier for that customer to do business with a firm.

Precisionaire's Bill Beck says there are flaws in the sytem of "Just In Time." Since the vendor often has to go in and rent warehouse space in a public warehouse, and must carry additional inventory, this cost must be built into the program. One way or another, the cost has to be paid. While the customer may save in handling expense, he will face a certain increment in his product cost.

When a company conforms to JIT requirements it is, in effect, working in partnership with its customer and must call upon its own vendors in the partnerships they have established to also bend their practices to meet the requirements.

Steve Wikstrom of Minnesota's Reell Precision Manufacturing says he sees few of his customers going to a true "Just In Time" system, though he feels his company would be ready to meet those demands.

"Really big companies are just not sophisticated enough to handle JIT," says Wikstrom. "Instead they seem to deal with a 'safety stock' mentality."

Does the need to meet customer delivery demands create quality problems? John Irace, CEO and vice chairman of Packaging Concepts, Inc., manufacturer of custom packaging for various food products nationwide, says certain products cannot be rushed.

"We've had times when customers want our product right away, but there is a specific process which includes letting the product cure which can't be circumvented," says Irace. "This can't be compromised to speed up delivery. When this happens our sales representatives have to explain this to the customer and give them alternative delivery times which can still ensure product quality."

Nevertheless, says Irace, prompt delivery is a part of customer service and the successful company must consistently meet those customer needs. When special demands arise, his company seeks assistance from suppliers to rearrange schedules, expedite delivery of raw materials, or whatever can be done within the parameters of product quality to meet the customer's needs.

Inventory management and rapidity of turnover is an element of quality management which centers on good asset utilization.

Beck says focusing on inventory management causes companies to pay attention to training in the shipping and receiving areas which is often ignored.

"We want each warehouse to be like a grocery store where it's all labeled and you have overflow so the home location is not disturbed," says Beck. "This way you cut down mistakes and have a better handle on true needs."

At Atlas Bolt and Screw, in Pennsylvania, Sales Manager Joe Stager says management of raw materials and machine usage is a key to their profitable operation. To this end they make extensive use of charting, entering usages based on past history and seasonal needs.

When volume fluctuates, adjustments are made accordingly and, when the chart falls below a certain level, additional material is ordered for the plant.

At Packaging Concepts everything starts with scheduling. Purchasing determines how long a lead time will be required. Since everything in their operation is custom ordered, excess inventory can lead to problems because the materials they have on hand are treated for printing and can go bad if left sitting in storage too long. A schedule board keeps track of everything with magnets. All equipment usage is scheduled as well as customer due dates and dates when material is set to arrive. This visible means of monitoring deadlines keeps customer and product demands in front of everyone's eyes.

As the marketplace for mature products tightens and competition heats up with more and more vendors, it becomes increasingly difficult to pass along the costs of higher inventories and "Just In Time" services to customers. The marketplace allows customers to view this as an expected service and if a company is not willing to meet those needs, someone else may be willing to step up and do so.

Here is where quality management, in terms of developing partnerships with customers, can work to everyone's benefit. As has been pointed out in earlier chapters, in a quality partnership the buyer and seller look at the overall cost of a product or service and the buyer views the health and long-term viability of the seller as a necessary component of that partnership. When this occurs, the emphasis begins to move toward a "fair" price rather than low price. To this end, becoming a "quality" company may provide a solution to the "beating up on price" which seems to be escalating in so many industries.

Nevertheless, meeting those customer expectations will require better and faster inventory management.

"I see a trend to quicker turnover and tightening up on vendors," says Beck. "Performing to specifications will be emphasized more and more. One of these specifications is getting the product there on time. This is not exactly JIT, but it's close!" ●••

37

Quality And The Sense Of Urgency

Do it now! The customer is waiting! Opportunity is slip-ping away!

It could often be said of established companies, "If we keep going in this direction we'll end up where we're headed!"

People tend to focus on the next short period of time (the upcoming months or weeks, for example). The fog rolls in and they may lose a sense of urgency that comes because they don't see that their current direction will take them to loss of market share or bankruptcy. People need to see that what they do this Tuesday will affect what will happen one year from now.

Don Kardux often uses nautical terms in his consulting work with his Business Navigators firm. He reminds his clients that the larger the ship, the more time it will take to turn around. This means that the organization has to predict what lies ahead. Its people need to have a sense of urgency to see far enough ahead to take action in a timely manner.

How does one go about generating a sense of urgency?

"You yourself have to see the results of actions you are taking today," says Kardux. "Visit the future. Get out and taste it. After you have witnessed the failure or success that lies ahead over the horizon, communicate this to your key people so that they come to believe they need to change and that they can change."

"In effect you say, 'You won't have to worry about coming into work at seven a.m. if this continues—there won't be a building here!' "

Jim Wall, president of Quality Business Forms, Inc., says symptoms of a lack of urgency include very visible things such as late deliveries, complaints from customers, quotations not being delivered on time, and lagging sales volume.

The organization lacking urgency may be characterized by complacency and the employees' lack of interest in the actual functions of what the company is doing. The heart of the quality process is said to be pride of ownership. When the people doing the work don't have any pride in their product then it's time to turn things around.

There are many reasons why people lose heart. Sometimes it is external conditions of the economy. It is easy to reflexively blame management and, indeed, management can do a lot to set the tone. In the early part of this century, blame was always placed on the workers, but the fact is that this burden must be shared.

We take away some of the pride of workmanship when we put the burden solely on management. They cannot own the process entirely. We have to say to people, "I don't think you're doing things properly. How can we help?"

Wall says it is the responsiblity of the CEO to constantly monitor what employees are achieving and lead them to what is expected. It may well be necessary to sit down face to face, one on one, to explain the things that need to be done for success and help the worker understand that if he is successful then the company will be also.

Once a company falls into the doldrums it can be difficult to pull back out, but not impossible if there is a commitment from everybody on down the line. Consultants have told me tale after tale of companies where the whole atmosphere began to perk up as management began to open up communication. We need to help the employee who thinks nothing will change to come to a firm conviction that change is and will be occurring.

Does the sales department, with its customer orientation and aggressive posture, bear a special responsibility to communicate this sense of urgency?

"It's dangerous to give communication with the customer to any one division within the company," says Kardux. "Everyone can and should be communicating with that customer. Surprisingly, the people closest to the customer in most organizations are the clerical and financial people who regularly talk to customers about invoices and bill payment. Accordingly, we may need to piece together a patchwork of skills with people wearing marketing hats, customer service hats, and looking for opportunities wherever they may be."

When a company institutes a formal quality improvement process it is important that the managers and facilitators joining the effort communicate the need for urgency in implementation, as well as all of the little daily tasks that collectively consitute quality service.

If the manner of presenting the process and the steps taken in the initial days are lethargic or lacking in inspiration it will be no surprise that the process itself reflects that casual and uninspired start.

Do it now . . . do it right the first time . . . and make sure the efforts don't let up! ●●•

38

Quality And The Entrepreneur

The start-up company faces unique challenges in conforming to the requirements of quality, yet it may be the easiest situation in which the owner or manager can guide and control development of a quality culture.

Why is it important for the start-up company to focus on TQ?

"The key to any company starting out is consistency," says Jim Wall of Quality Business Forms, Inc., which he started in the 1970's and which still bears his personal imprint today. "If you're consistent people will have confidence in your business!"

Wall likens this to purchasing a hamburger at a McDonalds. You know it's going to be the same in New York or Tuscaloosa. There are no surprises and you know exactly what to expect.

"We use computer programs on customer re-orders which store specifications so there is consistency for the customer," says Wall. "We don't change printers or other factors frequently and our customer service people work with customers to ensure there are no deviations."

Out of one-hundred people who start businesses, some ninety will fail. Generally this is blamed on undercapitalization but it often is a result of the entrepreneur's focusing on survival instead of doing things right the first time.

Any company starting out is under stress and quality is an elixir to solve these problems. Quality is one thing that doesn't cost and if the company can do twenty per cent of the right things they will probably get eighty per cent of the results.

"Since quality has no up front cost," says Don Kardux, "it helps focus on that twenty per cent of actions needed. In effect it condenses what needs to be done and acts as a short-cut to success. It will help you comprehend which twenty per cent will give you results and can save you some of the time invested in the other eighty per cent."

The start-up company has a number of advantages in establishing a quality process. People are dealing directly with the owner and have the comfort of knowing they are going right to the top. That owner, at least initially, has total control of everything. If he is totally committed to quality that will stamp the company's early efforts. As the company grows, however, the owner must be able to delegate and will have to focus on training to maintain the levels he has established.

The new company does not need to break bad habits. There is no culture to change and the workers can be brought into sync with the owner's philosophy from the very beginning. In large companies, a good percentage of the time in the early stages of a quality process is spent just getting the employees to stop what they're doing to focus on the effort. This is the proverbial "kicking the mule to get his attention."

The disadvantages of the beginning operation include the fact that there is no proven track record and customers must be convinced that a company will perform the way it says it will. Confidence will have to be earned. A great deal of this can be resolved by the confidence and skill of the owner if he is a good salesperson.

"The customer doesn't care where he buys," says Wall. "He is dealing with a salesperson and counts on that person to provide what he needs."

Kardux says new companies sometimes suffer from their lack of experience in failing. They inadvertantly get into difficulty without realizing the consequences of their actions.

This is illustrated by a story he tells about the different manner in which pioneers on the American frontier and Indian tribes taught their children to be careful in handling fire.

The pioneer mother would continually warn her child to stay away from a hot fire. Time and again the child would crawl up to the fire and be pulled away by the mother who would say, "No, No—Hot!" The Indian mother, on the other hand, would watch silently until the child went up to the fire, stuck his or her hand in, and began to scream in pain. "No, No—Hot!" said the squaw. Experience gave the words meaning.

Are there systems which should be implemented right from the start? Wall stresses the importance of having a competent CPA who can project and forecast and make sure the company is on track financially. The owner should work closely with the banker to ensure good cash flow and also with the person in charge of credit and collection.

"Good communication with these three people can allow the principal to devote his efforts to selling and marketing," says Wall.

Kardux feels it is important to put a plan together based on determining where the company would like to be at a given point in time and then "travel backward."

"The tendency in planning is to start by saying that in a year you want to be at a given point and then think about what needs to be done tomorrow," he says. "We need to be thinking about what we need to be doing at given points in the future (say ninety days, six months or two years) rather than just the next day or week."

"If a person wants to get from point one to point ten it is easy to start at one and then go to two, three, four. Sometimes it's better to start at ten (three months from now) and then look at nine (two months), eight, etc. Look behind to see what it will be like."

If you do "backward" thinking you can see the time it will take to realistically reach your goal.

Quality can be viewed pretty much the same way whether an organization is a sales or manufacturing entity. It again is a focus on the little things which, put together, make a package of first class service or products.

Wall does note that quality is monitored differently in different kinds of businesses. Some time ago his sales company purchased a small printing plant.

"In an active manufacturing process you can walk out into the factory and make sure the quality is there before it's shipped," says Wall. "In sales it all comes back to communication. In fact, in all kinds of businesses, if you are communicating frequently and clearly with the proper people there should not be quality problems."

As the enterprise grows, the closeness to customers and the hands-on charcteristics of the start-up company can begin to fade. How does the quality company keep this from happening?

Kardux says a key is the development of systems (repeatable by anyone in the organization) to ensure a company is listening to its customers. He cites an example of a "bug card" used by one of his clients which they place on their counter and in their invoices on a postage pre-paid post card. It tells the customer, "All of us are committed to improving quality," and then allows the customer to complete sentences such as, "It really bugs me when . . . ," "You'd receive more of my business if . . . ," and, "Your employee really helped me when . . ." and similar questions.

Kardux also agrees with the celebrated concept of "management by walking around" to ensure that managers interface with their internal customers.

"You must also get face-to-face on a regular basis with your external customers," he says. "Get in the car and go see them!"

As Wall's company grew, he instituted a regular series of monthly meetings to ensure all key people in his organization were on top of developments affecting customer service. A different employee each month heads up the meeting, making an agenda and deciding what needs to be discussed and what problems require action.

The entrepreneur is the kind of person who is naturally oriented to risk-taking. Perhaps it is this natural orientation that suits him and his organization to the quality process. He or she will not be wedded to a rigid way of doing things or a narrow way of looking at problems.

For some, the risk inherent in a new enterprise becomes focused on a fear of failure.

"That very fear is the paralyzer that stops people from centering their efforts on quality," says Kardux. "It's difficult to see the results of a quality process at first and sometimes people are so caught up in survival and fear that they are not able to turn their attention to the right things. An example of this might be where the impact of not receiving a customer's check on time puts the company at risk of having to close its doors. Here they may be focusing on the results of a lack of quality (the invoice not being paid) rather than the faulty system which caused that to happen."

The start-up company has all the advantages. They approach the total quality process with a clean slate.

The confident entrepreneur generally has all the tools to keep his company on a quality course as long as he establishes good systems and doesn't try to go it all alone. "If you feel confident that you could successfully work for anybody else," says Wall, "why not work for yourself?"

Total Quality—doing it right the first time—may be the key to getting the start-up company off the ground! ●●•

39

*Temporary Employees
And The Quality Process*

At the same time the Total Quality Movement began to gather steam in the late 1980's and early 1990's another phenomenon became prevalent in the workplace. Companies were increasingly using temporary workers to match their staffing to the fluctuating needs of the market.

The drawbacks to this were that workers seeking the security of permanent employment often did not realize their goal and the company, while saving dollars up front, might well find a depersonalized work force without highly developed skills applicable to the specific job. A company intent on pursuing "quality" might find it difficult to bring temporary workers into the process and integrate them into the developing quality culture of the organization. In fact, the presence of significant numbers of temporaries could be seen as detracting from the unity and common purpose which should ideally characterize the workforce involved in a Total Quality effort.

Integrating the temporary worker into TQM at an enterprise, while difficult, is not impossible. If the work is properly structured and a company acts in partnership with the temporary help firm, it can create an environment where the temporaries become active and equal participants in the process.

An example of successful blending of temporary workers and an active quality program can be found at Reell Precision Manufacturing in St.

171

Paul, Minnesota. This manufacturer of components for office equipment and laptop computers employs an average of twenty to twenty-five temporary employees per day.

Starting up in 1970, the company focused on quality from day one, a process which has become more formalized in recent years as the company has grown to its present 110 employees. With a significant portion of the workforce composed of temporary workers, the company spends a unusually large amount of time in training and orientation activities.

"We conduct an extensive initial orientation for these workers," says Vice President of Manufacturing Steve Wikstrom. "This focuses on three goals—safety, quality, and productivity."

After signing a non-disclosure agreement, the employee is placed in a self-directed work team. The production work force is split into these teams with full responsibility for their areas including the authority to call for more temporary workers. After taking part in an orientation, the temporary employees are included in all general company activities.

"We have a culture that sends a subtle, but clear message to these workers," says Wikstrom. "The message is that we are concerned about people and products."

Wikstrom credited much of the success of the arrangement to Manpower Temporary Services which has worked in partnership with them in securing personnel. He said that Manpower spends a significant amount of time one-on-one with managers and supervisors at Reell and does an effective job of screening people to determine adaptability to the company's requirements.

One of the factors which particularly suits Wikstrom's business to temporary employees in the quality process is the company's short-cycle production time. Only two minutes elapse from beginning of production of an item to its final testing. There is always a mixture of permanent and temporary people at each job station and function and these people are rotated from station-to-station regularly.

Manpower Temporary Services, the world's leading provider of temporary personnel, is committed to delivering quality training and integrating employees into existing Total Quality programs, says Sharon Canter, director of strategic information for Manpower, headquartered in Milwaukee.

Canter says her company surveyed three constituencies to determine customer expectations in the area of quality. These three groups are: (1) customers; (2) temporary employees; and (3) Manpower's professional staff. Surveys were conducted in the United States, the United Kingdom, and Canada.

Customers reported that their basic expectations were that the temporary employees have the necessary skills, report on time, be free from absences, demonstrate confidence and fit into existing work groups. Flexibility and willingness to take on extra tasks were also cited as key expectations.

Workers who are viewed as exceeding expectations are those who take initiative to resolve problems, ask questions, demonstrate understanding, and leave notes and instructions for the next employee.

The upshot of this research was the development of a Service Quality Training program for the Manpower workers. The program is being offered to all employees in all locations.

"Our own quality training is a point of beginning," says Canter. "After this we work as a team with the client company. We orient the worker—right from the start—to the client company's specific quality initiatives."

Canter says that Manpower service representatives work with the client company's human resource and quality control people to ensure that everything flows smoothly. Manpower continues the process with regular visits to the company as well as ongoing assessment of workers' performance.

Manpower's temporary employees are frequently included in customers' quality circles and process improvement programs. They strive to send the kind of employees who are able to grasp the existing culture of the workplace.

Manpower has established its own quality programs for internal use and a "Quality Performance" program which allows them in a systematic way to survey customers (both client firms and temporary workers).

"We look for trends," says Canter. "We have integrated this information internally and share it with both customer groups so that there is a feedback loop."

Training and commitment to a quality philosophy alone will not ensure success for temporary workers. Accordingly, Manpower utilizes a series of skill assessments which measure requirements common to various jobs such as ability to follow instructions, attention to detail, desire to do quality work, and speed. Task-specific tests measure more finite skills such as the ability to spot product defects and the use of tools and blueprints to assemble objects. In addition to testing the skills of light industrial workers, skills of office workers are tested as well.

The commitment to quality systems and procedures prompted Manpower to achieve registration to ISO 9000. In the registration process auditors review the complete operations of a company including policy and management responsibility, process control, control of non-conforming product, and documentation.

Manpower's first step in this process was the successful registration of nearly 200 offices in the United Kingdom and Israel. Manpower's 1000 offices in the United States and Canada are in the process of applying for registration.

Consultant Dave Gleason of Systematic Selling, Inc., points out that it is difficult to go back and renew training of temporary workers in situations where there is high turnover.

"It's tough enough to keep new employees on board," says Gleason. "Quality is expensive for long-term employees. With a long-term payback, it may be difficult to justify the training investment in temporary workers."

This is all the more reason, says Canter, that temporary help firms must become involved in training. They need to assume responsibility for coordinating the integration of the worker into existing quality processes. This can best be accomplished by ongoing partnerships with client companies, she says.

At Precisionaire, Inc., in St. Petersburg, Florida, Quality Manager Bill Beck says the company's permanent employees are encouraged to be supportive of the seasonal workers his company employs. This is something that is stressed as part of the company's employee involvement programs.

"We try to provide extensive training for these seasonal workers before they actively begin the job," says Beck.

What is the biggest problem encountered in bringing temporaries into the quality structure?

"The baggage workers bring with them from previous experiences," says Wikstrom. "It's a shock for some people to be brought into an environment where they're trained, equipped, and trusted."

Wikstrom observes that some workers who are assigned to duties at his company have never been asked for their opinions and ideas and some are very uncomfortable with this. Also, the peer pressure for quality work and productivity may be foreign to their experience and may require time for them to adjust. A small percentage never do warm up to this type of culture and soon move on.

"We have a firm belief that everyone wants to do their best," says Wikstrom, "and here they have an opportunity to contribute and share in the rewards."

Reell worked with the local Manpower office to develop wage structures to reward the temporary workers for success within the company's quality objectives. The primary source for hiring permanent employees is the pool of temporary workers.

It is not impossible to carry out a Total Quality process with large numbers of temporary workers. When both the client company and temporary help service are focused on integrating workers into quality and the job lends itself to rapid orientation, this process can work. The problem is that this is not always the case and as companies turn more and more to temporaries they run the risk of building a work force detached from the ongoing company culture. Some academicians and workers' advocates are decrying this corporate shift to what they call "disposable workers."

In some respects there is a basic inconsistency in the rise of the Total Quality movement and the departure from traditional concepts of career employment and company loyalty. With TQM's constant emphasis on building a company "culture" one wonders about the real impact of shuffling people into and out of that culture.

From a positive standpoint, the growth in temporary jobs has provided an outlet for those seeking careers with flexible scheduling to meet family or other needs.

With both quality and the rise of temporary employment seemingly the waves of the future, some means of reconciling the two must be found. This reconciliation probably lies in the development of a pervasive quality culture throughout American industry, not just specific to given enterprises. Loyalty to standards of quality and excellence might take the place of the company loyalties of the past.

Those companies that combine the best of both worlds—an effective Total Quality culture with the flexibility provided by temporary workers—can gain a competitive advantage. It will work only, however, where real attention is paid to ensuring that the needs of workers for security, benefits, and recognition are addressed. ●●•

40

*The Family Business
And Quality*

Tradition is an important concept
at many of the family businesses
which once were the mainstay of our economy and which still play an
important role today. Long before the quality movement became recognized as an entity unto itself, traditions of quality products and service
were handed down from parent to child as family enterprises made their
way in the marketplace over the years.

The family business embarking on a TQ process faces unique problems. Nevertheless, it possesses certain advantages which can enhance the
quality experience.

Where the family business has long operated with vague and extemely
informal lines of authority, or where the all-powerful founder has run the
business in an autocratic manner, the culture change required for Total
Quality Management may come as a real shock. There may be an aversion
to formal meetings and clearly defined procedures which will be necessary
to make the program work. Also, since the history of relationships
amongst the leaders of the business is longer and deeper, the negative baggage people bring with them is much more powerful. On the other hand,
if family relationships have been good and are characterized by open communication, then leaders of the business can give each other the support necessary for success.

"When relationships are good in a family business they are very
good," says consultant Don Kardux. "When they are bad they are horrible!

What Tom did to Bill twenty-two years ago carries a great deal of weight today."

Nevertheless, the advantages a family business carries in dealing with TQ may well outweigh the negatives. Families are generally unified in philosophy because they come from the same background and training. If the principals of the company are disposed to quality all participating family members will probably fall in line because they are of the same basic mind set. Further, the authority structure in such an enterprise tends to allow for quick action and a fast and clear decision for quality after management is exposed to the idea. The family provides a cadre of leaders already in place who are able to network the philosophy throughout the company.

The quality concept may be particularly appealing to the leaders of such an organization because oftentimes their name is on the door and family and personal pride can provide an impetus for building a reputation for quality. Who wants the family name to be associated with shoddy work and discount pricing?

Perhaps one of the biggest advantages enjoyed by a family business is the ability to focus on the long term rather than on the next quarter's profits. For many such companies, surviving from one generation to another is the goal rather than instant profits. The quality process is ideally suited to companies able to see things from this long-term perspective.

"The principals of the family business are working toward a common goal," says Bob Barnett of London Metal Services, Inc., a family owned distributorship in Ontario.

"You have to approach the quality process without setting a specific time line," says Barnett. "The idea is to get better and you can become frustrated by looking at things from too narrow a point of view."

Family enterprises may be based to a large extent on personal relationships and loyalty from employer to employee and from company to customers. These relationships fit in nicely with the concept of serving internal customers and meeting the expectations of external customers.

"Commitment from the leaders of the business is key," says Kardux. "The dynamics are different in each situation and the facilitator or consultant should look to determine who is the leader of the family. Who do they follow?"

This same search for the prime influencer characterizes the process even in non-family businesses. Sometimes people don't recognize who the leader in the business is but they still follow him or her.

Gaining the commitment of active family members may start with a "family meeting" to gain support of the concept, stressing the role of leadership and the example family members must present. There can be an appeal to family pride and the question can be asked, "What do we stand for?" This can backfire, however, if it starts the process with a sense of exclusion of non-family employees and managers from the process.

Non-family managers must be encouraged to develop a sense of ownership in the process by early involvement in decision making and by appointment to high visibility positions. Kardux stresses the importance of clearly and visibly recognizing when the first outsider makes suggestions.

"It's not enough just to use the idea," he says. "Reinforce this with recognition such as 'what a great idea!' But this must be sincere and real."

Oftentimes we do not state the obvious, but to provide proper recognition and impetus to participants it is important to call attention to active involvement and ideas.

Institution of formal quality may serve to "professionalize" the family business. For the first time the difference between a real meeting and one over the coffee pot or the breakfast table may become apparent. Quality standards may provide a source of leveling and even-handed applicability of procedures which may have been lacking. In a family business, while logic would say standards should be applied evenly, it may be difficult where the boss is also a parent and where family members may have very different work ethics. Where this exists it can lead to discontent among both family and non-family workers because of the clear imbalance.

Kardux notes that there are unusual situations where, for personal and family reasons, a member of the family who is unable or unwilling to conform to standards may be retained in employment. In such instances he suggests the family leader should address this problem directly with key employees stating the direct personal reasons why the individual is being retained or the performance is being tolerated. Where in private counsel a father says, "I'm trying to save my son and I need you to continue to work with him," most people will accept this. Where such a problem is ignored or not addressed people will begin to view the whole situation as one from which they must escape.

The steering committee for the TQ program should include family and non-family members and their representation should correlate to their involvement in the company. This may mean that there will be disproportionately more family because they are in positions of responsibility. They should not be ignored just because they are family as this would be as unfair as excluding all non-family employees.

Frequently the family business founder has become accustomed to ultimate power. The delegation inherent in TQ and the trust which must be placed in subordinates will help to break this down. The founder, if he truly embraces the concept, will grow from this transition also.

"Such fiefdoms are created by nepotism, blood, or longevity," says Kardux. "Non-family people can create this too, but there is a tendency for family members to believe they possess authority and act autocratically when they have not earned the right to do this. An example might be a twenty-three year old given the role of sales manager over a seasoned sales force."

This is where even-handed application of standards can help not only the business but the growing and developing young family manager who will have to conform to expectations and, if successful, will gain increased self-respect.

The ownership family itself perhaps has the most to gain by turning to TQ in the business. Not only are the ultimate rewards increased profitability and continued perpetuation of the business, but the communication skills and concepts mastered, such as goal setting and conflict resolution, can carry over into the family and personal life.

"I have seen the consultant's role evolve to family counseling and ministering," says Kardux. "Because the focus is on the business rather than the personal side of life, there is not so much of a threat, but the members can learn ancillary skills which can be applied to personal and family conflicts. Happiness is always a by-product of some other process."

"TQM's effect on a family business situation depends on the rule system in the family," says psychologist Patrick Openlander. "Every family has rules, often unspoken and unconscious, about every aspect of its functioning. These rules govern decision making, parenting, how affection is expressed, how new information is integrated, and how new rules are made."

Openlander says these rules express the structure of the family at a profound level and they would certainly determine whether the processes and insights of TQM are used. In those families that allow new information to be accepted and integrated, TQM has the potential to be exceedingly helpful to the family in many of the same ways it helps a business.

"Role clarification, good communication and morale could all be positively affected," says Openlander.

The process can help people in the family to appreciate each other and what they each bring to the party. The initial evaluation period as you start a program is very important as people begin to understand the contributions various family members can make or are capable of making, as well as other people in the business.

To get the process under way, an outside facilitator should meet with the family in an informal environment to scope out the family baggage and feelings—what it was like as a little child in this family.

"This information has to be eased out with a feather," says Kardux. "You can't be too blunt because it is very painful. Without some understanding of these hidden problems, however, communication within the family and the business may never be opened up."

Just as with any business, the family enterprise will never be able to find a specific road map to quality. There isn't one.

"You have to reach into the long list of approaches to quality and pull out what you want to do with your business. It's okay to do it your way," says Barnett. "Take the time to get outside help, however, because such help can provide the needed objectivity to get to the heart of matters and speed up the whole process."

Total Quality and the family business—a concept which was around before today's quality movement—but one that can benefit from the application of today's more formalized approaches. With successful involvement in TQ the family business can continue to service customers for the next generation! ●●•

41

Overcoming Obstacles
To TQM

Despite increasing numbers of companies climbing on the Total Quality bandwagon, a close inspection will show a lot of them quietly falling off that wagon.

This is not so readily apparent because a fading quality effort will not be accompanied by the fanfare and press releases of a new undertaking and, perhaps, the managers and employees are not even aware that the effort has been abandoned. They just stop doing the things they had committed to and return to business as usual.

This quiet fading away is seen more often in small businesses than large. This is probably because the large businesses set up a bureaucracy to administer the program which has a life of its own and tends to perpetuate the systems and procedures which make TQM a permanent part of the culture. Small businesses, on the other hand, make the mistake of approaching it as a program with a specific life and, once a planned set of events has occurred, they become consumed with other pressing needs and the program is forgotten.

This does not mean that all hope should be abandoned. Periodic renewals of quality can help to energize a process and, if done properly and at reasonable intervals, can keep the process in the forefront of everyone's mind.

Nevertheless, programs do tend to come apart when certain things occur. Let's take a look at some of the more common problems and see what might be done to head off difficulties before they sink the quality ship.

Lack of Management Commitment

Over and over again, this is cited as the number one cause for failure. Since commitment is an intangible thing, one has to look at the actions of management to see whether they can be altered to give clear evidence of that commitment and send the proper message to the employee-partici-pants.

"The greatest barrier to employee acceptance of TQM is management's untimely response to steering committee suggestions," says Don Kardux of Business Navigators. "Top management must be involved and believe in the process and failure to even respond to the concerns of committee members will discourage further creative thought."

Kardux suggests a two-week response time limit be set up to ensure that answers will be returned. These answers may not always be a straight yes or no but may contain modifying suggestions, possible new directions, or requests for more information.

At any rate, the response should show that the suggestions are being taken seriously.

Failure of Line Workers to Take the Process Seriously

This may stem from experience with other kinds of "programs" which started with great fanfare and faded away. Employees must get the message that this is something different and will permanently affect the way that they will approach their jobs. The importance of feedback cannot be stressed too much. Constant communication of results and improvement in performance should be communicated to the workers (number of pieces produced, defect-free products, error-free order picking, etc.). The goal is to make it possible for the employee to say, "I did this and I can see results!"

Reluctance of Line Supervisors to Get on Board With TQM

Quality starts at the work group level and the leader of that group must believe in and be committed to the process. This will only happen if he or she is allowed to be in on the development of the program and feels some ownership of the process.

"Training needs to be directed to these supervisors," says Bill Beck of Precisionaire, Inc., the national manufacturer of air filtration products headquartered in St. Petersburg, Florida. "Let them see what you're trying to achieve."

Beck says peer pressure can be used effectively to bring the doubter on board.

● Absence of Measurement or Insufficient Measurement

If total quality consists only of cheerleading and slogans and employees and managers are unable to assess if they are making progress toward stated goals the program is likely to run out of steam. Service businesses, in particular, have a hard time measuring success since their output is often very intangible.

Even if they can come up with measurements of desired output, getting a true reading on those kinds of things (i.e., service response time, customer complaint free transactions, etc.) is harder to track than defect-free products coming off of an assembly line. Also, the leaders of service businesses may tend to be less statistically oriented than their counterparts in manufacturing enterprises and may tend not to put sufficient emphasis on systems and statistical analysis. This calls for a disciplined approach which can bring other benefits to the business if conscientiously undertaken.

● Failure of Teams to Act Effectively

Action teams may be the heart of the employee involvement aspect of a quality program. They can fail if not given appropriate guidelines and clear expectations as to what they are to produce.

If there are "non-participants" on the team, perhaps they should be removed or reminded of the commitment they made when becoming part of the team initially. This underscores the importance of prior commitment which can be driven home by a pre-agreement, signed by all team members, outlining what is expected of them.

● A Perception that Time Is Wasted at Meetings and with Unnecessary Paperwork

Meetings and paperwork are a necessary part of TQM, but it should be viewed as productive time. Meetings in particular should be well planned with an agenda and a specific goal in mind.

Kardux suggests that paperwork can be kept down by use of a project board. Cards are placed on the board with one idea per card. They can be moved around rather than rewriting the ideas as priorities change. On the cards are tasks people have agreed they would do and management's response. With the projects on the wall for everyone to see there is a great impetus for management to respond.

External Pressures of the Marketplace

"Pricing pressure and pressure for lead times can be restrictive factors to quality," says Ken Urbanski of Haber Operations in Detroit. "The just-in-time approach sometimes gets a bit out of control. You need time to do things right."

How are these problems surmounted? Urbanski says they must be controlled with well-thought out procedures and an emphasis on partnership with customers where the parties are able to openly communicate about needs and capabilities.

Diffusion of the Message Because of Physical Separation of Worker Groups

Numerous people point to the difficulty of having a cohesive quality program where a company has geographically diverse branches.

In the wholesale distribution industry this is cited as a recurring problem. Branch operations tend to be very small and the branch manager has a great deal of autonomy because of his customer relationships and distant removal from authority. The imposition of a very structured program runs counter to the "free agency" which these managers often enjoy. There is a perception that, "We know what works here," which may be true to a certain extent.

Nevertheless, there are benefits to be derived from a company-wide quality drive and it can break down if certain locations are perceived to be exempt from the program.

I spoke with a representative of one large wholesaler who told stories of the company president "dropping in" and visiting at a distant branch the day after the branch manager had expressed resistance to institution of quality procedures at his location. The word rapidly spread throughout the organization and the many branches quickly got in line.

Inter-department Jealousies

This is another reason why leadership of the quality program must be chosen from among those with a company-wide perspective. If the process is seen as originating from a particular area (i.e . accounting or one particular product division) it may result in resistance from those who don't feel they will share in the glory from any success.

A general approach to this is to get nominal agreement to the process at the outset. If jealousies arise, go back to that nominal agreement, pointing out to the people that they made a contract and asking them "Why aren't we following it?"

Management Actions that Discourage TQM

Borderline decisions on rejecting parts and accepting less than perfect performance must always be resolved in favor of quality. Management must not send the message to "let it go" when employees know what's right and wrong. Tolerating substandard performance puts a damper on enthusiasm and sends the wrong message.

A Perception of Hypocrisy in the Quality Message

Both employees and customers must not perceive that a commitment to quality is made for public consumption only. If quality policies are published, brochures are distributed, and statements are made, then there must be visible follow-up in action.

If the whole process is seen as a public relations ploy or a means merely of pushing workers harder, then the process may produce more negative than positive results. Again, it goes back to management's sincerity of commitment.

A decision must be made to follow through completely on the quality process. Not to decide is to decide. Someone must own the plan and be the manager of the process. That must come from the top, regardless of the existence of a facilitator or day-to-day manager. Obstacles to TQM can be overcome, but the best way to overcome them is not to let them arise in the first place! ●●•

Reports From The Front Lines.
- -

Looking
Ahead

42

Quality And Education

Small business people know the problem well!

It's the counter person or truck driver who sees no need to present a businesslike appearance. It's the secretary who can't spell and who lacks an understanding of the rudiments of grammer. It's the clerical or warehouse worker who feels that a slipshod approach to a project is good enough as long as it gets by without rejection by the customer or management.

We all talk about quality, and we repeatedly devise programs to upgrade service levels and attempt to provide our customers with a top-flight product. At the same time, we deal with a pool of employee applicants who not only lack basic math, spelling, and language skills, but who see little relation between pleasing the customer and the continuance of their paycheck. What has gone wrong? What can be done about it?

Is our education system failing? Is it the disappearance of the traditional family, or is it the business environment itself that is creating the problem?

Undoubtedly all are contributing factors, but in this chapter we will focus on the educational experience we are providing our young people and ask why we are not demanding a higher level of performance from students and educators. Young people will have to spend some forty to fifty years earning a living, and if they do not master basic skills and acquire the proper attitudes and habits, they will be at a lifelong disadvantage. Our country will also fall behind in competition with those nations whose workers measure up to the task.

Alarm bells first went off years ago warning of declining standardized test scores. Since then various reforms have been instituted and additional funding has been made available for hundreds of studies and test projects. Despite this, if we look to test scores as a barometer, it is apparent that little has been accomplished with respect to improving the reading, writing, and computational skills of our students.

While per pupil spending in adjusted dollars rose from $3,500 in 1980 to $4,200 in 1987, student achievement varied little. The National Assessment of Educational Progress reported that nearly 60 per cent of 17-year olds lack the reading skills necessary to comprehend materials prevalent in business and higher education. In math skills, only the top five per cent of American students scored at the Japanese average.[1]

What does this mean for employers? It means we will be dealing with a decline in product quality and operating at a competitive disadvantage. It also means we bear an additional burden of providing remedial on-the-job training. If workers come to us ill-prepared, then we must devise programs to bring them up to speed or structure work responsibilities so that they can be handled by people whose basic skills are deficient. This is at odds with the increasing complexity of technology and the automation of the work place. There are simply fewer jobs for those with minimal skills. How do we get involved and make a difference?

Dr. James Boldt, a lifelong educator who served for many years as National Director of Elementary and Secondary Schools for the Lutheran Church-Missouri Synod (the nation's second largest network of church-affiliated schools), says business people can and should help create and generate an educational system which encourages competition and quality.

"Parents are crying for this," says Boldt. "They want their children to benefit from the educational marketplace's best efforts to create the best education for preparing their sons and daughters for contributions to the common good."

Boldt advises business people to "take on" schools that continue to espouse systems which create too many young people with a false sense of security. He charges that too many teachers are passing along an expectation to children that someone will take care of them, a current—but no longer acceptable—philosophy! This may result from the system in many schoool districts whereby the teachers are "taken care of" by others. No matter what their productivity, they still get paid and get raises and advances. This, says Boldt, must end.

There are four basic community pillars that, when functioning well, make for a productive society that serves the common good of each one of the four. These are:

1. *The homes in which people live, learn, love, and play.*

2. *The economic or business community.*

3. *The political community (city hall, police department, public schools, etc.).*

4. *The religious community (which also includes schools and human care institutions).*

In a utopian society, each performs a distinct function that informs and influences the others without hindering their specific roles and responsibilities. The business community is the primary consumer of our public and private school products, namely its graduates and its drop-outs. Boldt argues that the schools must take some credit for these drop-outs, even though the schools are working with young people who are products of what he describes as a "dysfunctional American media." This media has, by and large, belittled, scorned, humiliated, and ridiculed the institution of the family and the roles of mothers and fathers. This has been occurring for the better part of three decades and there seems to be no easing of the onslaught.

Given the power and influence of the media, is it any wonder that ordinary people have come to view their plight in life as one that should be free from family? Is it any surprise that they feel they should be free to pursue whatever course of life and action that makes them feel either good or fulfilled regardless of responsibilities?

"Right now," says Boldt, "most of those who wield the power of influencing homes and education are not influencing the common good very well."

When a city's water is contaminated, the city goes to great lengths to correct the problem. After all, people are sick and some are dying. Boldt asks, "Can we do less than find the problem and correct the situation in our educational system? I think not! There's a public trust at work here and the very value of the 'trust of the public' in the community and those leading it calls for, even demands, exemplary efforts to establish and maintain the common good."

Boldt calls for an end to the separation of the four community pillars described above in an effort to address the violence and misbehavior in our schools and our society. He recognizes that many might call this mixing church and state, but this viewpoint ignores the real benefits that could come from this interdependency. People in positions of authority must be more concerned about the "common good" than they are about their own positions.

Business people must become involved in ensuring we provide quality education because, quite simply, they are more committed to the common good than those now in charge of public education.

The teaching of values plays a number of key roles in quality education, one aspect of which is teaching the mutual obligation of employer and worker to deliver a good day's pay for a good day's work.

Boldt hearkens back to a principle passed along to him by his late father: "If you want it, you have to earn it!" Today, he senses an expectation that is 180 degrees foreign from this philosophy. Young people instead seem to feel they are owed something by society, be it schools or employers.

Values—true values—need the interlocking work of the four community pillars. Apart from values there is no education. In fact, it is impossible to have any quality education without this. Even poor education will be teaching values. Every time a teacher asks a student to learn or master something—anything—the teacher is saying, "This fact or truth is valuable." An educational system that avoids drawing lines between what is right and wrong in terms of behavior and conduct will be teaching values of doing "what you want when you want."

We are reaping the harvest of the teaching of the media that having things is more important than treating other people with respect and decency. A result of this is the drugs and prostitution that is rampant in our urban areas, says Boldt.

"You can bet these youths did not learn this from their parents or their churches," he says. "They learned it from the media which was not challenged by their classroom teachers."

Values are pursued because they are based on some sense of motivation. Generally, values serve a person's own needs.

Why would we want our employees to be honest? Obviously so they don't rip us off! Why would we want employees to be nice to other people? So the company gets more business and we make more money!

Why do we as employers want them to have a happy home and family life? So that when they come to work they perform well and, again, we make more money.

Just as the business owner must be honest with himself about his own sense of values, so must he understand the need for motivation and promoting a sense of values in workers (or students). Boldt suggests that among the key values to be imparted to young people by an educational system are the following:

1. *Putting others' interests before your own.*

2. *Doing everything possible to help people meet their needs.*

3. *Showing care for others by doing for them what you would do for yourself.*

4. *Helping anyone and everyone regardless of race, creed, or color in whatever need they have.*

5. *Listening to others so that someone really hears them.*

6. *Working for justice and love for the unloved.*

7. *Challenging those in high office to deal honestly and fairly with all.*

8. *Empathizing with those who have no advocate.*

9. *Sympathizing (but not pitying) with those who need our sympathy.*

There is a consistency in these values and meeting one's own needs while meeting those of the community and surrounding people.

"This motivation is the hallmark of good business," says Boldt. "It is, in fact, a paradigm. It is simply this—when I help others I end up profiting. Inversely, when I look out only for myself I end up failing. The whole thing is a paradox. If you want to succeed, you must meet people's needs. If you can think about the needs of others and help them meet these, you probably will no longer care about your own needs and things will take care of themselves."

With respect to basic skills, Boldt says successful businesspeople recognize the obvious. While not a businessperson himself, he has repeatedly heard the horror stories about young people coming to the workplace who are unable to follow directions, read a map, perform simple mathematical tasks, or speak effectively by placing a subject and verb together.

The U.S. Chamber of Commerce has established the Center for Work Force Preparation and Quality Education to start a national grass roots campaign for educational reform. The Center was founded on the theory that the most successsful and lasting solutions must come from the local level, spearheaded by business, education, and community leaders.[2]

One problem that has impeded progress is that professional educators and business people often do not speak the same language.

Educators tend to see problems in terms of concepts, and view education in a broader sense as opposed to the nuts-and-bolts straightforward approach of employers. Providing a forum to reconcile these different points of view is the role of intermediary organizations such as the Chambers of Commerce.

With some 2900 local chambers nationwide, many of which already have active education committees in contact with local school districts, the Center will attempt to provide business leaders with the information and the tools needed to act as catalysts for change.

This program will include attempts to develop a national campaign to link business, education, and community leaders together to stimulate active reform. It will identify successful programs and show local business leaders how to get them underway. It will develop issue papers on various topics from the viewpoint of what employers need students to learn, devise informational programs to inform young people of the economic benefits of completing their education, and will gather and maintain a database of education contacts in member chambers nationwide.

Given the skill levels of applicants we often deal with, it is apparent that business people have little choice but to become involved. We will either solve the problems in the schools or wrestle with the problems in the workplace.

We need to be in constant communication with educators so that they can understand what is required on the job. We must provide moral and financial support for those educators and legislators pushing for real educational reform, not just tinkering with the existing order.

If this means speaking up for tough options such as longer school days, fewer holidays, or public scrutiny of standardized test results—so be it!

This also means working to make sure educators are compensated fairly while at the same time weeding out those who are failing to get the job done.

A quality education is the ticket to allow a person to travel the road to pursue the American dream.

"The genius of this dream," says Boldt, "is simply this . . . become part of us, benefit from us, make a contribution to us, and live and die by the quality of your contribution and your handling of resources. But never, never think that our openness is a license for you who think you can get anything or everything for nothing. That will not and cannot ever happen. For to even hint at that would be to deny that we need each other, not as leeches, but as contributors to the common good." ●●•

43

Quality And
The Moral Imperative

Some have said "Quality is its own reward."

There is a sense of right and wrong in everything we do and, to a certain extent, a business has an obligation to produce quality goods and deliver quality services by the mere fact that it is holding itself out as being in business.

"Quality may be said to have a 'moral' dimension insofar as those who depend upon the organization (its clients and customers, as well as its employees) depend upon its survival," says Powell Woods, "and its survival is a function of the quality of its goods and services."

Woods, former vice president of human resources at Nestle USA, views this from the unique perspective of one intimately involved in the top levels of corporate planning who left to pursue an education in theology and who currently serves as pastor of a church in Cleveland, Ohio.

"The primary moral obligation of any management team," says Woods, "is to focus the employees of the organization upon quality and to assist them in every possible way to carry out the quality mission."

A true organization-wide dedication to quality does a great deal to improve, in very substantive ways, how employees feel about themselves. A large part of anyone's self-image is contingent upon how he or she feels about life at work. Work is, after all, quantitatively the largest single element in our lives. Most of us spend more time and emotional energy on our work life than on anything else.

"Our work life is a composite of what we do at work and what others do as well," says Woods. "In fact, what we do is to a very large extent determined by what others do. This is another way of saying that each employee is immersed in his or her workplace culture and that the culture pretty much sets the limits and determines the nature of the employee's contribution."

Woods says that while there may be a few "phenom" exceptions, no employee will continue to "slug it out" in order to deliver top-quality performance in a workplace culture that has become a swamp of mediocrity.

"Where the passion for excellence has turned into the soup of indifference," says Woods, "the vast majority of employees will just swim around, trying to keep their heads above the soup line."

Psychologist Patrick Openlander agrees that working for a company bent on delivering quality goods and services positively affects worker self-esteem.

"Workers thrive in an atmosphere of realistic demands and high achievement," says Openlander. "Identifying with a successful organization naturally promotes pride and TQM provides a special boost to this pride because it gives workers a deeper sense of ownership in the outcome of their efforts."

To be included in decisions, to be asked opinions and find that their ideas count, to have a chance to provide direct input to supervisors all increase self-esteem. This is built through competent performance and recognition by supervisors and co-workers. A successful TQM program will promote these values and productivity will typically increase in the midst of such an atmosphere.

Stan Hurt, president at Indiana Supply, says that people prefer to see themselves as employees of a high quality and high ethics company.

"Employees are looking for a company they can believe in," says Hurt. "Our company has been profitable by following this philosophy. We have grown and have been able to maintain our margins by continually trying to deliver what we promise and emphasizing this to both our employees and customers."

This moral responsibility for quality rests squarely upon the leadership of an organization. While it is possible for a de facto quality process to come from within the ranks, it is certainly difficult without leadership. If employees remain unconvinced that their management cares about quality it becomes almost impossible for them to pursue it in any meaningful way.

"There are just too many things that managers can do—or not do—day to day and month to month which can sabotage quality to just leave it to the rank and file employees," says Woods.

He says it is not a question of motivation, for most employees possess a great deal of potential for being motivated on behalf of quality, as much as it is a question of realism. Nobody wants to be a "bullet hitting a gelatin mold" day after day, says Woods. While a true quality workplace culture does primarily consist of diligent day-to-day efforts on the part of rank-and-file employees (i.e., doing the little things right the first time), all those diligent efforts must be coordinated and unleashed by managers who oversee production and interface with customers. Woods sees this not so much as a hierarchical issue as much as it is a "sequential" one. The last person to see the product disappear into the hands of the customer and the person who will deal with the customer should the product be defective, is generally not the same person who stamped the part or put the product together. The result is the great dependency of the rank-and-file employee upon the management, sales, and customer service parts of the organization.

"If this does not imply moral responsibility attendant upon those parts of the organization," says Woods, "it is difficult to see what would!"

Hurt says management does not always have control over quality levels. Decisions are made by line workers whether management is promoting quality or not and these decisions will impact upon the company's performance for its customers.

"If employees are interested in the success of their company, they will recognize that quality is a result of each employee's performing his mission correctly."

"If everyone does it right the first time," says Hurt, "there will be a synergy throughout the organization."

Does quality go beyond the workplace, spilling over into the private and community lives of workers?

"Sure," says Hurt. "That's part of our program. We feel it should apply to home life as well as work. The skills of communication, listening, and making good decisions are applicable to the ways people relate to their families, friends, and how they deal with life situations."

Openlander says that successful TQM increases the likelihood that workers will see themselves as valuable, which can improve their homelife in several ways. They may be encouraged to treat family members with dignity in the way they have been treated at work. Additionally, TQM can carry over at home through improved problem-solving skills, more patience in trying to understand others' point of view, and the ability to model confidence that comes with success.

Does the growth of the quality movement have relevance to the moral standards of a nation?

Woods notes that Tom Peters has been stomping around the country for many years saying that quality is a moral issue for our country as well as for individual organizations within it. Nations are now organizing themselves to compete internationally.

"We obviously do live in a global marketplace and have no choice but to compete," says Woods. "The question is, how best to do this? The answer should be obvious. It is free enterprise, pure and simple, which has produced the greatest economy and largest market the world has ever seen—not government assistance."

There are implications here for concepts of industrial policy, insofar as such concepts include mixing up government in the affairs of private companies at the level of business planning, competition, strategy, and operations. Woods argues that here, as elsewhere, the most valuable contribution government can make is to ensure free and unrestrained marketplaces and provide for the common defense. The rest should be left to the free exercise of trade and the ingenuity and the hard work of private companies.

"Most American companies know by now that quality is an effective strategy for survival and growth," says Woods. "Let them go forth and do it!"

Openlander says that the success of societies can be measured by the degree to which they succeed in providing their members with meaningful work. In this sense, those who direct our institutions have a responsibility to provide structures to link people's work efforts with suitable meaning.

Quality as a moral issue? Yes.

There is a moral price to failed quality. That price will be paid not only by material failure of the business but by the managers and employees who must deal with the inconsistencies in what they do and how they wish to perceive themselves. ●••

44

Quality And Growth

The great success stories of American business, if we judge by notoriety and media coverage, are not necessarily the conservative, yet profitable businesses that have stood the test of time. Our attention is drawn magnetically to the "shooting stars" of the world of commerce—those companies who multiply their sales and market share, branch offices, and employees in rapid succession.

This may be a result of the American fixation on "bigger is better," but it does have an exciting appeal and the top talent of the business world always seems to gravitate toward these fast-moving enterprises.

With the recession of the early 1990's came a realization that not all growth was good nor does growth inevitably lead to profitability. Along with this also came a renewed emphasis on quality, which manifested itself in the TQM movement.

Does rapid growth conflict with a focus on quality?

Russ Broeckelmann of Coastline Distribution, Inc., in Sanford, Florida, says there is a natural symmetry between quality management and growth which requires the multiplication of individual talents and the development of talents of others. "You must be in an atmosphere of growth to keep this process going," says Broeckelmann. "You won't get top quality with robots and to attract the kind of talent you need you must have growth. If you don't have it these talented people will take off for greener pastures!"

Honeywell's Jim Widtfeldt points to 1993 Baldrige winner Granite Rock Company, which he says was built on the basis of the Baldrige criteria, and has experienced rapid growth under this philosophy. Widtfeldt asks why we don't all base our businesses on these criteria since it should naturally lead to growth. Look at Microsoft, Apple, Saturn, and other high growth companies. They feature quality products and defect-free delivery. They have cultures supporting extraordinary performance in an atmosphere of rapid growth.

The extent to which quality and growth are complementary may depend on the stage of the product life cycle and the complexity of the product. If it is in the very beginning of product introduction and the product is simplistic then growth can drive quality and vice versa. If it is more complex then it can be a self-defeating strategy to grow fast. It can catch up with you and will result in quality problems because there will be a lack of managerial depth and experienced human resources.

What management practices can be used to ensure total quality service in the midst of rapid growth?

Widtfeldt says he is continually tempted to go back to the Baldrige criteria—leadership with vision and values articulated. Planning and good information systems tell management what's going on. Effective use must be made of human resources and results should be measured so that a company is not "pulling its own leg."

"Stay close to the customer," says Widtfeldt, "and try to keep short cycle times so new products go to market faster."

Broeckelmann says the key people within a company must come together to decide what needs to be done in any functional area of the business and consensus must be achieved on the missions and goals and the broad parameters of how these will be achieved in any area.

"With your team you have to set the basic platform for design of systems and strategies," says Broeckelmann.

As companies grow, quality depends to a great deal upon uniformity of standards throughout the expanding networks of offices, stores, or warehouses. It is important to have information systems set up before growth occurs so that progress of the new branches can be monitored. If the critical information is flowing to the right people then a problem can be caught in the early stages.

Broeckelmann ties this need for good information back to the initial planning of systems and strategies, focusing on what management feels is important to accomplish. How these strategies are to be implemented and how they are to be measured is key. An example would be a warehouse person who makes continual mistakes because of a user unfriendly system. When he or she is given a user friendly system then the warehouse person, as well as management, is able to monitor progress and improvement will result.

Expansion stimulates a constant need for staffing. With a constant flow of new people, how do we ensure that managers and employees are quality oriented?

Widtfeldt says we must hire for a quality orientation and continue to train and educate our people. This means trying to determine the degree to which an applicant is willing to take ownership of the company in his or her own job.

Broeckelmann says companies should promote from within whenever possible but should be prepared to hire outside when inside talent is not available. He would look for three criteria in staffing positions for quality: (1) Intelligence (which you can't teach); (2) Initiative (there just isn't time to follow a new employee around); and (3) The ability to get along with people (without this the first two don't matter).

Keith Dierberg of Concordia University says staffers in a growth organization should be selected based on criteria which correlate with quality employees. "If the best employees are left-handed and this has been proven then that's what you must look for," says Dierberg. "A lot of companies have criteria but they don't check the performance of employees selected to validate whether these criteria predict success in their particular business. These companies must stop to measure whether the factors on which selection is based are important in their own business."

With TQ's emphasis on meeting customer needs and expectations, certain benefits can flow from rapid growth. If customer convenience is of prime importance, more offices can increase customer satisfaction. An example might be a car rental company. If, however, the consumers are purchasing a product for consumption then the main advantage of dealing with a growth company may be the cost savings resulting from economies of scale. If a distribution system is critical, however, the more distribution points available the greater will be the customer's satisfaction.

Widtfeldt draws parallels between a growing organization and a living thing. In fact, he points out that the word "organization" comes from "organism".

"In this analogy," says Widtfeldt, "the information processing becomes like the nervous system. It has the role of sensing what's going on and interpreting what is happening within the other systems."

Most big organizations are cumbersome and bureaucratic. They are wasteful of resources because they rely on centralization, i.e. the head gets in the way of the body. Widtfeldt predicts organizations of the future will become more like coral reefs—a collection of cells that decided to get together. This will be manifested in groups of teams who have their own agendas within the general parameters set by management.

In the growing organization, says Widtfeldt, the notion of smallness or closeness or intimacy must stay alive. Groups welcome new members, orient them, and give them a sense of where they belong.

In a successful organization people own their own jobs, know their customers and serve them. Training of these new people becomes even more critical when a company is growing and the faster the growth, the longer newcomers need to spend in training and orientation. This is because all of their peers are busy or are new themselves and cannot pause in the midst of activity to pass on company philosophy.

A growing company faces a number of pitfalls which can derail its quality effort. Dierberg cautions about not having systems in place to assure delivery and consistency. He says the company also must have come to its own definition of quality and conveyed this meaning clearly to existing and new employees.

Broeckelmann says quality is needed before you can expand since it lays the foundation in the form of good systems and procedures. "Just talking about quality—what I call the 'rah-rah!' approach—will get you in trouble!" he says.

Widtfeldt cautions against taking a short-sighted or myopic point of view based on the misperception that customers are standing in line waiting for us to sell them. This is precisely what kills the golden goose! Big companies are now in trouble because they haven't had to worry about the customers and have forgotten that customers are the source of growth.

A growing company must focus on the idea of giving something back. In an environment of fast growth it's easy to ignore the basic source of prosperity—the community and all that it entails (the arts, charities, government, etc.). A company rushing ahead and not pausing to give something back is bound to fail. The growing Green Movement may force more and more companies to face up to the question of what they have done to contribute to society.

Growth and quality may complement and sustain each other or, if the company does not lay the proper groundwork, may prove to be mutually exclusive. It's all in the approach management elects to take and their willingness to do the necessary homework to prepare for expansion. ●●•

45

The Quality Renewal

Thereafter comes a time in the midst of every company's quality process when the effort begins to run out of steam. This may seem inevitable to those who have seen management programs come and go over the years and who, at first glance, may look at this as one more fad.

The general consensus that quality must be a permanent institution at a company gives rise to the necessity of providing a periodic "shot in the arm" to long-term efforts.

What are the signs that such a program is needed?

Consultant Dave Gleason lists the following symptoms of a program in need of rejuvenation:

1. *There is very little sign of an ongoing process.*

2. *Management perceives there is a low degree of awareness of quality amongst the employees.*

3. *Management feels somewhat depressed that nobody is grasping the quality process.*

Gleason suggests taking the company and its employees through a structured review of the basic steps in the quality process. His consulting firm approaches the revitalization process over a twelve to sixteen-week period concluding with an extensive workshop. During this period the internal/external customer surveys are repeated and the results are evaluated during the workshop. Emphasis is on understanding the process and prioritizing items for correction.

When employees leave the workshop they hopefully will have a fuller understanding of the process and its implications for the long-term health of the company. This differs from the initial exposure to TQM which may be centered on merely enlisting initial employee support.

Why is a periodic renewal necessary?

Most company managers attending training programs and seminars introducing the quality concept come away with expectations and aspirations that exceed what is truly needed to implement a process.

After six months to a year they often begin to feel that they have failed. In actuality they probably didn't fully implement the process by getting everyone at the grass roots level involved.

Renewing the quality process can be a difficult thing for management which may perceive initial efforts as a failure and reinstituting the process as merely "going back to the well" of an earlier embarrassment or defeat. Surmounting these feelings is a major challenge to the CEO who is still committed to the process.

One means of gaining support for this renewal process is membership in what may be described as "focus groups" of companies at similar stages in the TQ process. This may develop from "alumni" groups of specific quality seminars or training programs.

Russ Broeckelmann, President and CEO of Coastline Distribution, Inc. in Florida, recalls his days as a consultant where he served as facilitator for these kinds of groups.

"Methods, successes, and failures were discussed," says Broeckelmann. "Even failures turned out to be successes as we looked at them through different perspectives. Sometimes beauty is in the eye of the non-beholder! When we are close to a program like this it is apparently very easy to become too self-critical."

These groups give people a chance to compare notes with other "survivors" of the process. As war stories are shared it becomes apparent that there are as many ways to go after quality as there are people. The focus groups renew interest and provide support to those trying to rejuvenate the process at their respective businesses.

"After you have been through your initial attempts at TQM you are a whole lot smarter in your approach to the process and realize the pitfalls which can shortstop your efforts," says Broeckelmann.

The focus groups generally list twenty or thirty common problems encountered and several people are asked to explain how they handled these problems. Certain members of the group may be asked to make presentations of their company's quality implementation process touching specifically on some of the agreed upon problem areas. A brainstorming session follows for adding on and improving upon solutions and ideas.

One of the biggest problems in jump-starting the process again is the fact that employees may be cynical due to perceptions of early failure. The CEO and quality managers need to develop thick skins to work through this period until a fuller acceptance of the process can be achieved. For this reason the leader/facilitator must feel a deep commitment himself or herself, and the focus group can be helpful in pumping up courage to get in there and keep slugging away.

Additional devices to pump fresh enthusiasm into the process could include bringing in an outside motivational speaker, changing the structure of the process in some way to add variety, or instituting small incentive programs to highlight specific areas which need attention.

Does changing direction or emphasis help the renewal process or does it send the message that the initial effort has failed and create an impression that management is grasping at changes to "save" the program? If the thrust of efforts is to help employees more fully understand the nature of TQM then change should be seen as a positive thing. It is one more bit of evidence that the company is a living and growing entity capable of responding to change and that management is willing to make adjustments dictated by the reality of circumstances and experience.

When industries hit hard times and the wolf is at the door—when wage and salary increases are few and far between, when lay-offs are a fact of life—might not this add to employee cynicism about TQM? Why didn't it prevent all this difficulty?

Communication skills of management become critical in helping workers to see that poor quality would have and certainly will compound the situation—and that delivery of quality goods and services is the best way out of hard times!

If quality is indeed a process and not a program, management will have to deal with the inevitable high and low points which occur in every business. Recognizing that these swings in fortune will happen at every business regardless of their commitment to quality can provide reassurance to those who unfairly have judged themselves failures.

It could probably be said that the only true failure in the quality process is the company whose management has given up and is not willing to put themselves and their enterprise on the line! ●●•

46

The Quality Action Plan: Forty Things To Do Now!

So—where do we go from here? Where does one start the process or how do we get back on track if our quality effort has slipped off course?

Throughout these pages people on the front lines have shared their thoughts and opinions with us, stressing the things they feel are most important in the quality approach to running a business. As we have noted, the TQ process will vary from company to company. Each individual manager will see certain key elements as having more weight or value than others. Nevertheless, there are certain concepts and key directions towards which all companies can strive.

I submit the following forty points which, serving as the framework of an organization's efforts, will surely take the company to a higher plane of meeting customer expectations and set it firmly in the direction of Total Quality service. They represent a composite of the thoughts shared with us by the many people interviewed in this book. I am aware of continually falling short of these objectives in our work at Brauer Supply Company, but recognize their universal application and, hopefully, we will keep slugging away at the process of continuous improvement.

These principles are:

1. Define quality for your organization and develop a written statement of commitment.

2. **Recognize the importance of leadership. Be an evangelist for quality. Make the commitment yourself and determine to lead by example.**

3. **Develop a cadre of quality leaders who understand the importance of quality, the process, and have the ability to communicate these things.**

4. **Teach all employees at all levels to be customer conscious!**

5. **Choose a consultant or outside advisor with hands on experience in quality improvement. Make sure he or she is philosophically compatible with your company culture or that your culture is prepared to change to a new philosophy.**

6. **Set quality-related goals. Monitor progress toward their attainment and modify them as needed.**

7. **Ensure that the structure of your company keeps decision making close to the customer.**

8. **Empower employees to take control of their work processes within parameters clearly set by management. "Management sets the rules of the game and the workers call the plays."**

9. **Utilize quantifiable methods of charting and monitoring performance and progress towards goals, but be sure to blend this with human interaction and communication.**

10. **Work tirelessly to communicate to all employees the need for and methodology by which quality results can be attained.**

11. **Be open to change! Welcome things that upset the apple cart and look for opportunities there.**

12. **Make decisions based on input from all parties to be affected by decisions and then implement those decisions quickly and decisively.**

13. **Invest time and resources liberally in training employees in quality service and methods.**

14. **Be flexible and willing to change course without letting your own ego or those of other managers get in the way.**

15. **Promote a quality culture by seeking an emotional commitment which goes beyond mere systems and procedures.**

16. Find out what your employees think about your service levels by means of surveys and one-on-one interviews—keep the communication flowing.

17. Everyone in the company should be part of the sales and marketing department and should understand the concept of selling value added service as a part of the quality process.

18. Focus on doing the little things right the first time.

19. Devote time to ensuring accuracy and attention to detail for all goods and services provided.

20. Actively utilize developing new technology, but be sure it integrates with your overall efforts geared to meeting customer needs and expectations.

21. Strengthen partnerships with suppliers and those who ultimately help you meet your customers' needs.

22. Hire for quality, using available tools to assess predisposition for service, high energy, and a passion for excellence. Seek out those traits which have been proven to correlate with success in your own particular business.

23. Teach your people the concept of the "internal customer" and involve everyone in improving specifics of service to these internal customers.

24. Encourage the airing of conflicting ideas and encourage your people to seek constructive compromise.

25. Utilize data processing to bring into clearer focus the areas which need attention and improvement.

26. As employees are given ownership and control of their work, so must they also be held accountable.

27. Bring employees at all levels—even part-time, contract, or temporary workers—into your quality process by keeping that process simple and providing for immediate feedback.

28. Periodically step away from the daily routine and evaluate where you are headed and where you need to go.

29. Seek out successful companies in your field or outside your field and emulate their methods and techniques, striving to meet and exceed their performance levels.

30. **Recognize and reward your people for success in quality and exceeding customer expectations.**

31. **Share information with other companies in the TQ process outside your product or geographic markets. Join focus groups to exchange ideas and experiences.**

32. **Lay the foundation for quality— good systems and procedures—before you grow, rather than after the fact.**

33. **Apply quality principles to management of your assets, including inventory, and realize that having the right products and delivery on time is a prime factor in meeting customer expectations.**

34. **Establish teams of employees to identify and solve problem areas. Act quickly on the recommendations of these groups.**

35. **Apply the quality concept to your personal and private life and help create a climate where your employees can do likewise.**

36. **Give back to the community, which is the source of your company's prosperity, by devoting time and resources to community betterment.**

37. **Work for reform in our educational system to encourage teaching of quality values as well as improvement in basic skills.**

38. **Repeatedly renew the quality process, taking your employees deeper into understanding what it is all about each time.**

39. **Visit the future! Decide where you want to be by a given point in time and then plan how to get there and know where you need to be by specific points in time.**

40. **Strive to maintain a sense of urgency throughout your organization.**

Do things now, not tomorrow!

Conscientiously applied and assimilated into your personal and corporate value systems, these principles should help to keep you on course as you work to make your organization a quality enterprise.

Effective application of these guidelines requires that someone or some group of people within an organization must make an emotional commitment to lead the charge. If an organization can have dozens of people acting simultaneously on all of these fronts, then that organization will be well on its way to establishing a quality culture and becoming a living and growing entity.

Why not approach this in the spirit of the final principle set forth above. Do these things now—not tomorrow! ●●•

47

Looking Out
Across The Water—
The Future of Quality

The small sailboat leaned over in a steady breeze as we skimmed along the top of the blue waters of Whitefish Lake in northern Minnesota. I relaxed with my hand on the tiller and pointed the boat towards a spot on the far shore.

"Better watch what you're doing!" Bill Brauer warned me. "There's going to be a change."

I looked around and could see no sign of an imminent disaster and looked at him quizzically.

"Look over there," he said, pointing to the large expanse of water to our west. "See how the texture of the water is different. There's a strong breeze coming your way."

Sure enough, in about ten seconds, a strong gust took hold of the sails and pushed us forward in the slightly altered direction I had taken as a result of Bill's warning.

Over some fifteen years I learned much from the man whose position of leadership at Brauer Supply I now hold. Perhaps the most valuable lessons have been the analogies this avid sailor would frequently draw between running a business and handling a sailboat. If we wait until the wind changes, he would say, it may be too late. A strong gust will capsize us or we will fall behind the competition who anticipated the change. Perhaps worse, if we don't prepare to catch the wind we may find ourselves becalmed, sails slackened and dead in the water.

The skipper of any business, as with a boat, must keep his eyes on the horizon, looking for any change and planning what steps will need to be taken to meet any eventuality.

We have taken a look at the quality process as a set of specific steps to help a company deal with that change and have taken a look at its impact on many of the major issues and points of change facing our organizations today.

What does the future hold? How will the quality company evolve to meet challenges not yet even on the horizon? What of the future of the movement itself?

Russ Broeckelmann sees a greater partnership in the future between parties in the chain of distribution.

"Sam Walton taught retailing businesses new ways to do things," says Broeckelmann, "and he did it through a quality approach. We can't stop change but must adapt to it. We will have to ensure good communication with all partners in the chain of delivery and then it will get down to specifics for individual companies—doing things in a measured, quality way."

"If the quality concept is going to be living and truly meaningful it will have to grow to include how important and valuable people are," says Steve Wikstrom. "The way we treat each other at work will become increasingly important. If it doesn't then the whole thing will become unglued by self-interest if things get tight!"

Jim Widtfeldt believes the quality process as such will disappear, that it will become so much a part of the way we do business that it will be taken for granted.

"You don't ask people today whether they have telephones, faxes, or computers!" he says.

Widtfeldt believes we will see a similar intensification of technology and the role of human interaction.

"We used to try to reduce TQ to two separate schools of thinking—technology or the touchy-feely 'do good' side of things. This is the result of western thought where it's got to be one or the other—we can't see it as both."

Widtfeldt urges us to view these two aspects as two opposites coming together to create a greater whole. This is what we are seeing as people begin to talk about "integrated systems." We could draw an analogy to such things as day and night (different but complementary to each other) and men and women (very different but we have nothing until they come together).

The quality process can provide a structure and an impetus to take a business where it needs to go for survival and prosperity. A methodology is developing as well as a body of literature and a so-called "language of quality."

Do you want to know the big secret of quality?

Total Quality is not new! It is the same kind of process that successful businesses, organizations, families, and individuals have been undergoing for thousands of years.

When the ancients first developed systems of commerce there were winners and losers. Some people learned how to meet the needs of their fellow man. They did this consistently and with a sense of urgency. From generation to generation and from civilization to civilization those who did these things came out on top.

The secret is that there is no secret!

Do the things that we all know winners do and strive to do them better than anyone else. If you and your organization can achieve this you will have mastered the process of Total Quality! ●●•

Endnotes

Chapter One
1. Oberle, Joseph "Quality Gurus: The Men and Their Message," TRAINING, p. 31-36, January 1990.

Chapter Two
See "The Quality Policy—Getting It Down on Paper!" THE QUALITY OBSERVER, September 1992.

Chapter Three
See "Role of the Quality Steering Committee," THE QUALITY OBSERVER, August 1992.

Chapter Four
See "Setting Goals in the Quality Process," THE QUALITY OBSERVER, August 1993.

Chapter Six
See "The Quality Survey: Assessing Customer Needs," THE QUALITY OBSERVER, May 1993.

Chapter Seven
See "Employee Teams and the Quality Process," THE QUAL-ITY OBSERVER, April 1993.

1. Press Release, Rochester Institute of Technology, April 2, 1993.

Chapter Nine
See "Employee Empowerment and the Quality Process," THE QUALITY OBSERVER, January 1993.

Chapter Eleven
See "Aligning the Organization to Support Quality," THE QUALITY OBSERVER, June 1993.

Chapter Twelve
See "Selling the Quality Concept to Employees," THE QUAL-ITY OBSERVER, December 1992.

Chapter Fourteen
See "Partnering in the Quality Process," THE QUALITY OBSERVER, March 1993.

1. Paul Hyman, ELECTRONIC BUYER'S NEWS, November 1992.

Chapter Fifteen
See "Keeping the Customer in Mind," THE QUALITY OB-SERVER, July 1992, and THE SURPLUS RECORD, July 1992.

1. Peters, Tom, THRIVING ON CHAOS, p. 112, Harper & Rowe, Perennial Library Edition 1988.

Chapter Sixteen
See "Recognition and Reward in the Quality Process," THE QUALITY OBSERVER, October 1992.

Chapter Eighteen
See "Employee Training and the Quality Process," THE
QUALITY OBSERVER, November 1993.

Chapter Twenty-Two
1. Andler, Edward C., WINNING THE HIRING GAME,
Smith Collins Publishers, 1992.

Chapter Twenty-Three
1. From "Excellence Through Quality," p.10, pamphlet published by Southwestern Bell Telephone. Provided courtesy of
Mike Berry, Area Quality Manager of S.W. Bell.   Reference to Ishikawa, Kaoru, GUIDE TO QUALITY CON-
TROL, Asian Productivity Organization.

Chapter Twenty-Six
See "Quality Management-Repositioning for the Future," THE
QUALITY OBSERVER, June 1992

Chapter Twenty-Seven
For additional interviews relating to Quality and Technology,
especially as it relates to wholesale distribution, see Truesdell,
"Distributors and Technology: How Wholesalers are Coping," DISTRIBUTOR MAGAZINE, September/October
1993, and THE DISTRIBUTOR'S LINK, Fall 1993.

Chapter Twenty-nine
See "Does Labor Board Ruling Pose a Risk to Quality Groups?,"
THE QUALITY OBSERVER, February 1993, and "Qual-
ity Programs Under Fire!" in THE DISTRIBUTOR'S
LINK, Winter 1992, THE SURPLUS RECORD, March
1992, and DISTRIBUTOR MAGAZINE, February-
March 1992.

1. Electromation, Inc., 309 NLRB No. 163, 142 LRRM 1001
(December 1992).

2. Press Release from "The New Teamsters," Office of International Brotherhood of Teamsters, AFL-CIO, December 17,
1992.

Chapter Thirty

See "Quality and the Bottom Line," DISTRIBUTOR MAGA-
ZINE, July/August 1993, and THE DISTRIBUTOR'S
LINK, Summer 1993.

Chapter Thirty-three

See "The Growing Role of Corporate Security Management,"
THE QUALITY OBSERVER, November 1992.

1. Korpal makes reference to a study prepared for Chubb Insurance Group. See "Guidebook Helps Firms Curb Staff
Fraud," Windsor Star, p. A17, 9-15-90. Discusses Ernst and
Young accountants' publication of a guidebook on white-
collar crime for the Chubb Group of Insurance Companies.

Chapter Thirty-Four

See "The Drug War and the Fastener Distributor's Workplace,"
THE DISTRIBUTOR'S LINK, Spring 1992, and "The
Drug War and the Workplace," THE SURPLUS
RECORD, May 1992.

1. Drug-Free Workplace Act of 1988, 41 U.S.C. Section 701.

2. "Drug Screening and Job Performance—3 Year Study Shows
Link Between Drugs and Problems at Work," The San
Francisco Chronicle, p. B6, 12-5-90.

Column—"The Nation...in Brief" The San Diego Union, p. A-
14, 11-29-90. Reporting results of study which show those
testing positive for marijuana had 55 per cent more accidents
on the job, 85 per cent more injuries, and 56 per cent more
turnover than those who tested negative. Those whose pre-
employment tests showed positive for cocaine had 59 per
cent more accidents, 85 per cent more injuries, and 15 per
cent more turnover.

Chapter Thirty-Nine

See "Temporary Employees and the Quality Process," THE
QUALITY OBSERVER, October 1993.

Chapter Forty
"The Family Business and Quality," THE QUALITY OB-
SERVER, December 1993.

Chapter Forty-Two
See "Fastener Distributors and Education—We Have a Lot at
Stake," THE DISTRIBUTOR'S LINK, Winter 1992.

See "Small Business and Education...We Have a Lot at Stake!"
THE SURPLUS RECORD, December 1992.

1. For updated statistics and additional data see National As-
sessment of Educational Progress, TRENDS IN ACA-
DEMIC PROGRESS, National Center for Education
Statistics, November 1991.

2. Information provided from U.S. Chamber of Commerce,
Center for Workforce Preparation and Quality Education,
1615 H Street, N.W., Washington, D.C. 20062.

Index